# SOCIOECONOMIC SURVEYS FOR URBAN DEVELOPMENT AND WATER PROJECTS
## A GUIDEBOOK

NOVEMBER 2022

ASIAN DEVELOPMENT BANK

 Creative Commons Attribution 3.0 IGO license (CC BY 3.0 IGO)

© 2022 Asian Development Bank
6 ADB Avenue, Mandaluyong City, 1550 Metro Manila, Philippines
Tel +63 2 8632 4444; Fax +63 2 8636 2444
www.adb.org

Some rights reserved. Published in 2022.

ISBN 978-92-9269-786-0 (print); 978-92-9269-787-7 (electronic); 978-92-9269-788-4 (ebook)
Publication Stock No. TIM220433-2
DOI: http://dx.doi.org/10.22617/TIM220433-2

The views expressed in this publication are those of the authors and do not necessarily reflect the views and policies of the Asian Development Bank (ADB) or its Board of Governors or the governments they represent.

ADB does not guarantee the accuracy of the data included in this publication and accepts no responsibility for any consequence of their use. The mention of specific companies or products of manufacturers does not imply that they are endorsed or recommended by ADB in preference to others of a similar nature that are not mentioned.

By making any designation of or reference to a particular territory or geographic area, or by using the term "country" in this document, ADB does not intend to make any judgments as to the legal or other status of any territory or area.

This work is available under the Creative Commons Attribution 3.0 IGO license (CC BY 3.0 IGO) https://creativecommons.org/licenses/by/3.0/igo/. By using the content of this publication, you agree to be bound by the terms of this license. For attribution, translations, adaptations, and permissions, please read the provisions and terms of use at https://www.adb.org/terms-use #openaccess.

This CC license does not apply to non-ADB copyright materials in this publication. If the material is attributed to another source, please contact the copyright owner or publisher of that source for permission to reproduce it. ADB cannot be held liable for any claims that arise as a result of your use of the material.

Please contact pubsmarketing@adb.org if you have questions or comments with respect to content, or if you wish to obtain copyright permission for your intended use that does not fall within these terms, or for permission to use the ADB logo.

Corrigenda to ADB publications may be found at http://www.adb.org/publications/corrigenda.

Note:
In this publication, "$" refers to United States dollars.
All photos are from ADB.

On the cover: Well located in the Trapeang Prey village, Phnom Dey commune, Phnom Srok district, Banteay Meanchey province. Water supply and sanitation is a part of ADB-supported projects to improve accessibility to market and reduce transport cost, health and hygiene in Banteay Meanchey, Cambodia. The project has rehabilitated existing and constructed new wells, community ponds, and small community water supply system, benefiting 370,000 rural residents in six provinces. (photo by Chor Sokunthea).

# Contents

| | |
|---|---|
| **Figures** | iv |
| **Foreword** | v |
| **Abbreviations** | vii |
| **I. The ADB Project Cycle** | 1 |
| **II. Common Mistakes in Survey Questionnaires** | 4 |
|     A. Lack of Standardized Questions | 4 |
|     B. Too Many Questions in the Survey | 5 |
|     C. Disorganized Way of Asking the Questions | 6 |
|     D. Use of Vague Questions | 7 |
|     E. Use of Suggestive Questions | 8 |
|     F. Use of Absolutes | 8 |
|     G. Reliance on Memory | 9 |
|     H. Ignoring Cultural Differences and Sensitivities | 10 |
| **III. Identification of Core and Expanded Questions** | 11 |
| **IV. Pre-Survey and Survey Implementation Guidelines** | 14 |
|     A. Pre-Survey Implementation Stage | 14 |
|     B. Survey Implementation Stage | 23 |
| **V. Annotated Draft Questionnaire with Core and Expanded Questions** | 30 |
| **References** | 66 |

# Figures

1  ADB Project Cycle  2
2  Examples of Original and Revised Survey Questions  6

# Foreword

Socioeconomic surveys play an important role in project design. They provide useful information on the current situation in project areas and provide feedback on the acceptability and demand for the investment. Surveys are most often conducted at the preparation and appraisal phase to give an early indication whether the project is feasible or not. For this reason, developing high quality survey tools are of utmost importance to the Asian Development Bank (ADB).

Under ADB's Strategy 2030 Operational Priority 4, making cities more livable is our commitment to Asia and the Pacific. To this end, our Development Effectiveness Review estimates that the 2021 operations financed by ADB have delivered improved services to 50.6 million people in urban areas through 210 established or i mproved urban infrastructure assets, with 21 service providers upskilled with improved urban planning and financial sustainability capacity. In 2021 alone, ADB has improved urban environments, climate resilience, and disaster risk management in 18 zones in Asia and the Pacific and has supported 65 entities in developing member countries to improve their regulatory, legal, and institutional environments. All these accomplishments would not have been possible without the strategic information provided by socioeconomic surveys.

Against this backdrop, ADB's *Socioeconomic Surveys for Urban Development and Water Projects* was developed to standardize the questionnaires and survey approaches of ADB regional departments. It is a gender-sensitive modular questionnaire that allows project teams to customize sections of the survey instrument based on their project's outputs. Through a comprehensive review of internationally tested questionnaires, the guidebook offers project teams core and expanded questions for water supply, sanitation and drainage, and flood management surveys. It identifies common mistakes that survey teams should avoid to safeguard data quality and offers guidance on what to do before, during, and after data-gathering. The annotations in the guidebook explain how the different parts of the questionnaire come together and makes it easier for project teams to understand each component's purpose.

The coronavirus disease (COVID-19) crisis has posed significant challenges for ADB and other multilateral development banks in conducting surveys. Where applicable, this guidebook offers recommendations on how approaches can be modified to fit the new normal of pandemic-related restrictions on site visits, mobility, and social gathering. It also presents various technological alternatives to face-to-face surveys that maintain implementation efficiency while reducing the opportunity for errors.

This guidebook is the first of its kind in ADB, and was undertaken to promote knowledge sharing and capacity building across regional departments. It is a joint product of the Southeast Asia Department and the Economic Research and Regional Cooperation Department led by Aimee Hampel- Milagrosa and Thuy Trang Dang with the support of Dieldre Harder and Penny Dutton (consultants) under the guidance of Srinivas Sampath and Lei Lei Song. I personally hope that project teams, consultants, and resident missions alike will find it useful.

**Ramesh Subramaniam**
Director General
Southeast Asia Department
Asian Development Bank

# Abbreviations

| | |
|---|---|
| ADB | Asian Development Bank |
| CAPI | Computer-Assisted Personal Interviewing |
| CBA | cost-benefit analysis |
| CVM | contingent valuation method |
| ESI | Economics of Sanitation Initiative |
| FAO | Food and Agriculture Organization of the United Nations |
| FGD | focus group discussion |
| JMP | Joint Monitoring Programme for Water Supply, Sanitation and Hygiene |
| KII | key informant interview |
| MICS | Multiple Indicator Cluster Surveys |
| NGO | nongovernment organization |
| ODK | Open Data Kit |
| SDG | Sustainable Development Goal |
| SPADE | Spatial Data Analysis Explorer |
| UCCRTF | Urban Climate Change Resilience Trust Fund |
| UNICEF | United Nations Children's Fund |
| WASH | water, sanitation, and hygiene |
| WHO | World Health Organization |
| WTP | willingness to pay |

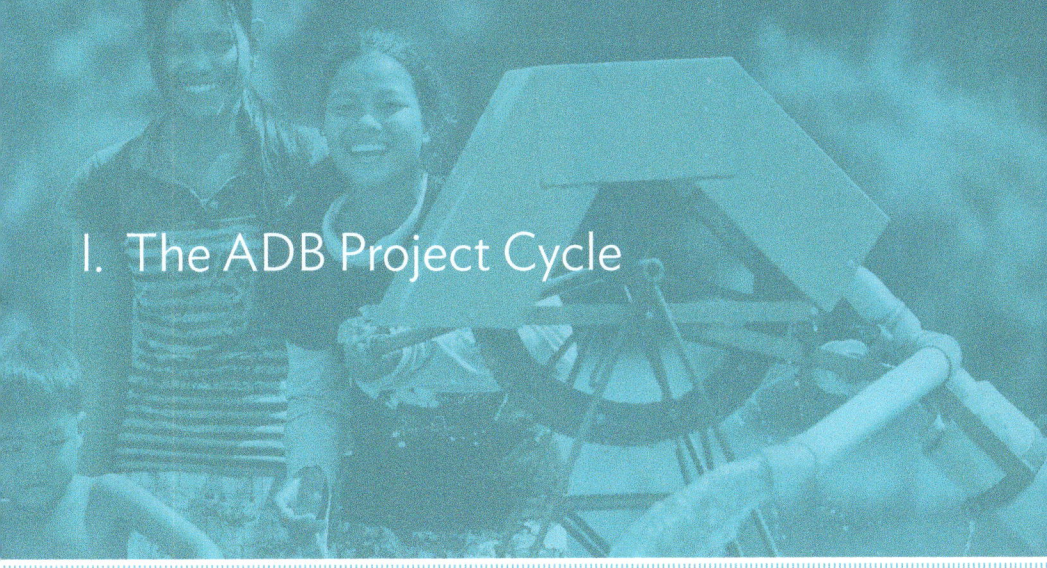

# I. The ADB Project Cycle

Socioeconomic surveys based on questionnaires are an effective method of collecting a sample of data from a target population. The data is then analyzed to describe the characteristics of the population, explain or predict a behavior or attitude, or to explore new areas of interest from which to draw conclusions and make important decisions.

For Asian Development Bank (ADB) projects, surveys can provide important feedback from people in a project area on the acceptability and need for a project, the current situation, their preferences regarding the project, the desirable features of project interventions, the project's affordability, and the people's willingness to pay for improved services. But, above all, surveys are significant because they give an initial indication of whether a project is feasible or not.

Surveys are most often conducted at the project preparation and appraisal phase of the ADB project cycle, especially as part of feasibility studies (Figure 1). Information obtained from surveys contributes to project design, and supports ADB's due diligence, which serves as the basis for loan approval. All projects that seek ADB funding are assessed during project processing.

Determining project economic viability through economic analysis is one of many due diligence requirements for ADB projects. Other requirements, such as sector assessments, the project's poverty-reduction and social strategy, risk assessments, climate change assessment, gender action plan, environmental examination, land acquisition resettlement plans, and financial analysis are also developed during the processing. Survey data is particularly useful for preparing the project's cost–benefit analysis (CBA). CBA establishes the economic viability of the project by measuring whether the estimated economic benefits outweigh the economic costs.

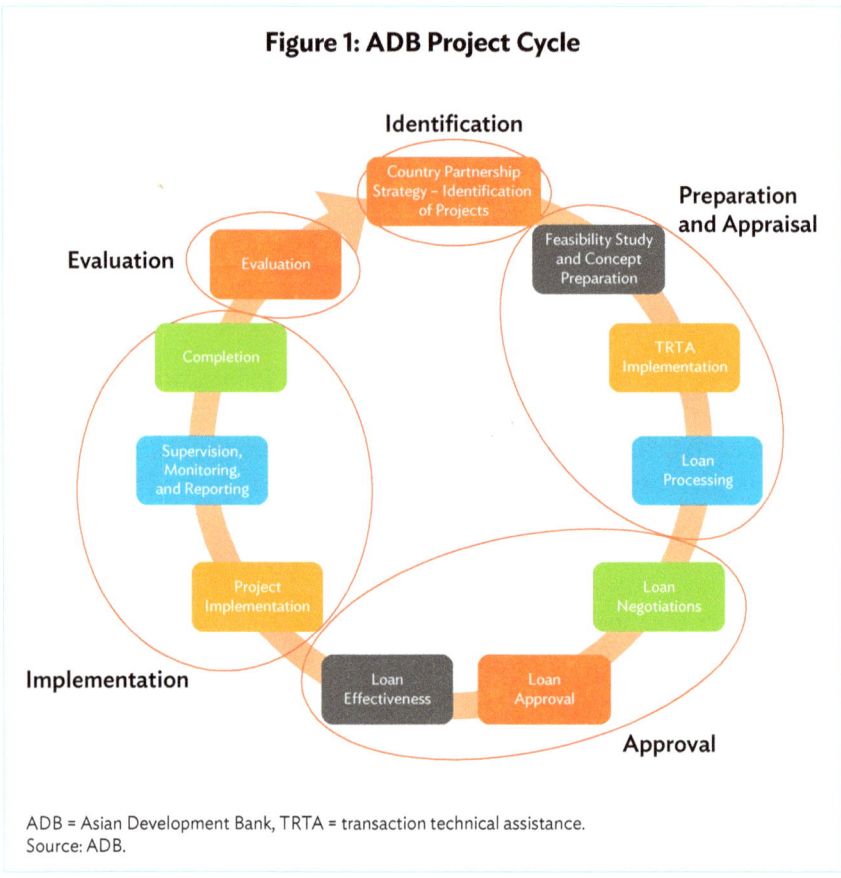

Figure 1: ADB Project Cycle

ADB = Asian Development Bank, TRTA = transaction technical assistance.
Source: ADB.

For example, ADB projects in urban development and the water supply sector support multiple outputs (e.g., house connections, sewer connections, garbage disposal, toilets, etc.). The potential benefits associated with these outputs are numerous and diverse, ranging from those that are easily identifiable and quantifiable in monetary terms to benefits that are intangible and difficult to measure. Differing benefits may also accrue to members of a household (e.g., women, children under five, or people with a disability).

The ADB *Guidelines for the Economic Analysis of Projects* (2017) provides instructions for assessing the benefits and economic viability of urban-development and water-supply projects. It identifies two general types of project benefits: incremental and non-incremental. Incremental benefits are derived from project outputs that meet additional demand, such as the construction of a new water supply or sewerage system. These benefits are usually measured based on the estimated consumers' willingness to pay (WTP) (in effect, the average demand price) for the incremental volume of water consumed due to a project intervention. Non-incremental benefits, on the other hand, are those arising from project outputs that replace existing supply (e.g., alternative sources for displaced water supply) and can be estimated using survey data. They are generally lumped into two categories: resource cost savings and health savings.

This guidebook on ADB urban-development and water-supply projects has been developed to provide practical guidance to project teams on good field survey design and implementation. It includes standardized questions and survey approaches for projects in the sector. The modular, gender-sensitive questions cover the core and expanded questions that project teams should include in their survey instruments to be able to estimate project benefits. Core questions, which are common to all sector project questionnaires, provide basic information on urban water and sanitation, and on solid waste and flood management, in a project area.[1] Standardizing core questions allows the comparability of basic data across projects. Expanded questions, on the other hand, include a larger set of questions that are intended to be used for more robust economic analysis, particularly in valuing project benefits and impacts.

The guidebook is structured as follows. Section II presents common mistakes in survey questionnaires that project teams should avoid. It presents a range of examples from various surveys to make identification of the mistakes easier, and proposes some alternatives. Section III identifies the sources of the core and expanded questions that are proposed by the guidebook. The sources are the urban-development and water-supply survey instruments of the World Health Organization (WHO)/ United Nations Children's Fund (UNICEF) Joint Monitoring Programme for Water Supply Sanitation and Hygiene, the World Bank, and ADB. Section IV provides pre-survey and survey implementation guidelines for securing data quality throughout the data-gathering process. Meanwhile, the annotated draft questionnaire with core and expanded questions is included in section V. The annotation clarifies what the questions are for and provides overall guidance to project teams.

---

[1] Core questions, however, need to be customized according to the scope of the proposed project (e.g., a water supply project versus an integrated urban project covering water, sanitation, and solid waste).

## II. Common Mistakes in Survey Questionnaires

Designing a good quality questionnaire is critical for ensuring that the data collected from the target respondents are accurate and reliable. It will also prevent erroneous conclusions and lead to interpretable and generalizable results. This section discusses common mistakes (SurveyMonkey n.d.; Hyman and Sierra 2016; Sullivan and Artino 2017; dataSpring 2018; Tonthat 2019) that project teams should avoid when designing survey questionnaires for urban development and water supply projects.

### A. Lack of Standardized Questions

Standardizing questions means using the same words or terminology when referring to a specific topic across the questionnaire. It also means including the exact same questions across surveys, using an identical format and response categories. Failure to do so leads to lack of clarity in the responses and in the meaning of the results, as well as inconsistency and an inability to compare the results of different projects.

Consider, for instance, survey questions on the regular maintenance of septic tanks. One questionnaire might ask respondents, *"How much does your household pay for desludging services?"* And another questionnaire may ask, *"What is the cost of the manual emptying fee?"* The second question may not enable an accurate calculation of benefits since the "emptying fee" could be interpreted as the cost per cubic meter of desludged septage instead of the amount paid by the household for the service as a whole.

This is also true for WTP questions on water supply, urban sanitation, and solid waste systems that are intended to capture incremental benefits. There are often notable differences in how the WTP questions are framed and in whether a contingent valuation scenario is included.[2] These differences can have a significant impact on the reliability of WTP estimates.

Using standardized questionnaires (i) allows a comparison of data, for example between baseline and endline; (ii) enables a comparison of results across projects; (iii) increases the reliability of standardized measures; (iv) makes it easier to communicate findings and interpret results; and (v) permits the generalization of behavior patterns (Garcia 2014).

## B. Too Many Questions in the Survey

Researchers may want to include as many questions in the questionnaire as possible in order to collect more data. There is, however, a trade-off between the length of the questionnaire and the quality of data and the response rate. Surveys that are too long, too complex, and too confusing can potentially lead to survey fatigue. Respondents who participate in these surveys may refuse to answer questions, provide nonchalant responses, or totally lose interest in completing the questionnaire.

An example is the inclusion of too many WTP questions. The respondent might be asked for their WTP for (i) a well-designed septic tank, (ii) improved fecal sludge removal services, (iii) improved sludge treatment, (iv) a piped sewerage system, and (v) clean and well-maintained public toilets. The inclusion of all the contingent valuation scenarios puts a heavy cognitive load on the respondents that may affect response quality and, eventually, the reliability of the derived WTP estimates. Value formation based on contingent valuation studies relies heavily on respondent comprehension and truth telling. If the respondent is intent on getting the interview done, instead of focusing on the WTP questions being asked, the responses may be compromised and, hence, may not be valid. It is suggested, therefore, that only one or two important contingent valuation scenarios be included in each interview.

---

[2] Contingent valuation (CV) is a survey-based method that asks people how much they are willing to pay for goods and services that are not usually bought and sold in the marketplace. Contingent valuation method (CVM) questions are often poorly framed. Most often, they do not include very specific details on project service improvements, which makes it difficult for survey respondents to accurately state their willingness to pay.

Given the time and effort spent by respondents in a survey, researchers need to identify and prioritize questions that are pertinent to their project objectives. This may include, for example, questions that are relevant in estimating the incremental and non-incremental benefits of urban-development and water supply projects. Meanwhile, unnecessary and redundant questions that do not contribute to survey objectives should be dropped from the questionnaire.[3]

## C. Disorganized Way of Asking the Questions

The way questions are structured and organized in a questionnaire is important because it can affect the reliability and consistency of the respondents' answers. It is advisable to avoid going back and forth during the interview, as that might confuse, overwhelm, or irritate the respondents.

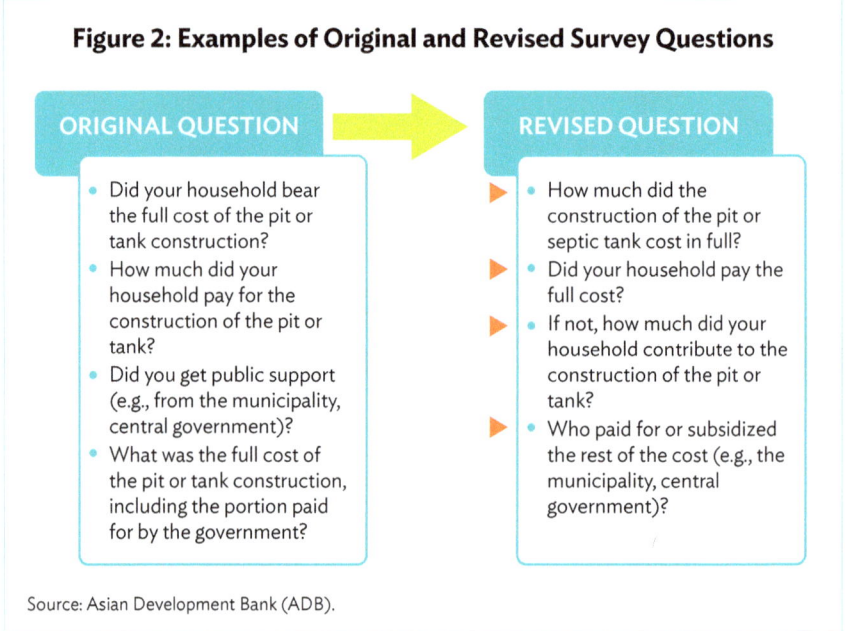

Figure 2: Examples of Original and Revised Survey Questions

Source: Asian Development Bank (ADB).

Figure 2 shows how questions relating to the cost of septic tank construction were rewritten and rearranged to improve their comprehensibility and logical flow. It is good practice to group related questions together and ask them

---

[3] In some cases, redundant questions are deliberately included in the questionnaire to help validate responses and to catch inconsistent answers.

sequentially because this will allow the respondents to focus on a single topic and to build their responses around it.

## D. Use of Vague Questions

A question is vague if it is not clear, specific, or well defined. It may be too broad or too poorly worded for respondents to have a common understanding of the question. Such questions may be open to the respondents' subjective interpretations, so the answers could be difficult to analyze. Some examples of vague questions include the following:

(i) **The use of words that may have multiple meanings**. The question, *"How satisfied are you with the quality of your piped water?"* may mean different things to different people. Water quality may refer to attributes such as taste, odor, and color. The result will most likely be inconclusive since respondents may be referring to different water quality attributes in their responses.

(ii) **Lack of a specific time frame**. Asking respondents, *"How much does your household spend on water?"* will most likely yield varied responses. Respondents may be thinking of their weekly or monthly water expenditures when answering this question. As a result, the data collected may not be valid or reliable.

(iii) **Incomplete and mutually nonexclusive response categories**. A range of response categories is incomplete if it does not cover all possible answers, including options such as "none of the above," "all of the above," etc. In addition, response categories that are not mutually exclusive will imply that there could be more than one possible answer, particularly for numerical ranges. Ambiguous choice options may confuse or frustrate respondents and produce incorrect results.

For example, the question, *"How often do you desludge or empty your septic tank?"* may have the following response categories: (a) every 1–2 years, (b) every 2–5 years, and (c) every 5–10 years.[4] This list of possible responses is incomplete because it does not include those who empty their septic tank at intervals longer than 10 years or who have never emptied their septic tanks. In addition, the choices are not mutually exclusive because the times overlap. Respondents who emptied

---

[4] There is often a confusion among surveyors and respondents on what a septic tank is. The terms "cesspit" and "septic tank" are often used interchangeably, resulting in distorted survey results. In many national censuses, this confusion led to inflated data on household use of septic tanks.

their septic tanks every 2 or 5 years could fall into multiple response categories, which could lead to incorrect results.

(iv) **The inclusion of two or more attributes in a question.** For instance, take the question, *"Is the public toilet facility safe and accessible?"* This question includes multiple attributes, but requires a single response. Specifically, it asks for the respondent's opinion regarding two different attributes of the public toilet: safety and accessibility. The respondent may be confused and provide an answer that refers to either the safety or accessibility of the public toilet facility or to both. The researcher might not know which attribute the respondent is referring to, and this ambiguity could complicate the interpretation of the data.

## E. Use of Suggestive Questions

A question is leading or suggestive if it subtly prompts the respondent to answer in a certain way. It typically uses an adjective that may provoke a respondent to give a biased response.

Take the following question, for example: *"Considering the importance of having a well-designed septic tank, would you be willing to construct a flush toilet with a septic tank as stipulated by the law?"* First, it assumes that the respondents agree that a well-designed septic tank is important. Second, it coerces the respondents into agreeing that they should build a flush toilet with a septic tank that meets the requirements of the law. The respondents are most likely to say "yes" to this question.

A neutral way to pose the question would be to ask the respondents if they are willing to construct a flush toilet and a septic tank with two chambers, etc. The question would simply describe the design of the septic tank as mandated by law without referring to the law itself. Neutral questions can generate unbiased responses, particularly on topics where the respondents are more likely to choose socially acceptable answers.

## F. Use of Absolutes

The use of absolute words such as "always," "every," and "often" in a question often makes the question rigid and inflexible, and may lead to a lack of variability in the responses. For example, if the researcher wants to ask the respondent, *"Is water always available from your main source of drinking water?"* and allows only "Yes" or "No" as response options, with only two possible answers, and given that "always" may mean different things to different people (e.g., all the time, most of the time ), this question will most likely generate an affirmative answer.

To collect information that will be more useful for analysis, researchers should expand the response options. In the example given in the prior paragraph, for instance, instead of only "Yes" and "No" options, the response categories could include (i) Yes, water is always available; (ii) No, water is available most of the time; (iii) No, water is available some of the time; (iv) No, water is rarely available; and (v) Don't know.

Alternatively, this question could be rephrased as, *"How many times in the past month has drinking water been unavailable from your main source?"* This wording would allow respondents to answer in a variety of ways, instead of forcing them to choose from a limited range of options that will not generate useful feedback.

## G.  Reliance on Memory

Respondents may find it difficult to recall prior events or behaviors, especially if they happened a long time ago. Questions that require respondents to remember events or behaviors in the past can generate inaccurate answers from the respondents, and thus compromise the quality of the findings. For example, past incidences of diarrheal disease among children under 5 years of age, along with the associated health expenditures, are easier to recall if they occurred 2 weeks before the survey, rather than 6 months or 1 year before.

Hence, for questions that rely on memory, it is better to use the shortest reference period that is consistent with project objectives. Another option is to use landmark events to aid the respondent's memory. For example, in questions about the damage caused by flooding in the past year, a reference could be made to a specific flood event or a typhoon known to have occurred in the area.

## H. Ignoring Cultural Differences and Sensitivities

Different regions can be sensitive about certain topics, such as income, water, sanitation, and hygiene practices. Ignoring cultural differences and sensitivities concerning these topics may undermine the effectiveness of the survey.

Potentially sensitive questions must be asked with care because respondents may refuse to answer such questions or provide untruthful responses. Asking sensitive questions about income, for example, will often lead to missing data or underreported values. To address this problem, income ranges may be used instead of more precise estimates, or consumption expenditure could serve as a proxy for income. Another way is to place sensitive questions at the end of the survey rather than up front. Respondents may find it less intimidating to answer sensitive questions after trust has been built and the purpose of the survey has become clear.

In addition, open defecation practices, anal cleansing methods, and menstrual hygiene management are often embarrassing topics to discuss. Residents may hesitate to disclose personal information for fear of being ridiculed. These questions need to be asked in a neutral way that puts respondents at ease and encourages them to answer truthfully.

Meanwhile, disregarding cultural differences may result in inaccurate data because some survey questions might not be culturally relevant or appropriate to the target population. For example, there may be questions that are prone to "yea-saying" because of cultural norms (Food and Agriculture Organization of the United Nations [FAO] n.d.).

# III. Identification of Core and Expanded Questions

To standardize the ADB urban-development and water-supply survey questions, the researchers adopted available standardized water, sanitation, and hygiene (WASH) indicators that are used globally. Questions included in surveys that had been administered by international organizations have since been accepted and applied by many countries in their national surveys. Standardized questions allow a country to report on its progress towards global targets—for instance, Sustainable Development Goals (SDGs)—and to assess its performance relative to that of other countries. Additional questions from regional surveys on water supply and sanitation were also considered, in order to capture the economic benefits used in economic analyses.

The references are described below:

**Joint Monitoring Programme.** The Joint Monitoring Programme for Water Supply, Sanitation and Hygiene (JMP), under the World Health Organization (WHO) and the United Nations Children's Fund (UNICEF), facilitates the global monitoring of SDG targets for WASH in households, schools, and health-care facilities.

The JMP developed core and expanded WASH-related questions for households. The core questions on water cover aspects of the households' drinking water supply, such as sources, expenditure, collection time, availability, and sufficiency. The core sanitation questions cover the types of toilet facilities, location, and whether the facilities are shared with other people. They also include basic questions on septage management, such as whether the septic tank has been emptied, who emptied it, and where the contents were disposed of. The core questions on hygiene include the availability of soap and water in the households' handwashing area, and menstrual hygiene practices.

A set of expanded WASH questions was also developed. For water, these questions cover water quality, availability, storage, and responsibility for water collection. For sanitation, they include shared facilities, accessibility, fecal waste management, and solid and liquid waste disposal. For hygiene, additional questions on handwashing and menstrual hygiene management are included.

**Multiple Indicator Cluster Surveys**. The Multiple Indicator Cluster Surveys (MICS) is a UNICEF-supported household survey program that started in the mid-1990s. Its purpose is to monitor the situation of children and women around the world. At present, it is being implemented across a wide range of countries and includes a complete set of tools, as well as technical assistance, for all stages of survey implementation.[5] MICS uses the core and expanded WASH questions from the JMP.

**Economics of Sanitation Initiative Regional Survey**. The World Bank's Economics of Sanitation Initiative (ESI) conducted a pioneering regional study of Cambodia, Indonesia, the Philippines, and Viet Nam that examined the impacts of poor sanitation on health, water, the environment, tourism, and other areas of welfare. The data used in the analysis were drawn from various studies, investigations, databases, and surveys.

The ESI household survey focuses on the transition from open defecation and unimproved toilet facilities to basic improved sanitation facilities. It includes questions that complement the questions from other surveys, such as those concerned with time savings in accessing defecation areas, resource savings from fertilizer and ash, and time and expenditure savings on health care, among others.

**Socioeconomic Survey for Urban Development and Water Supply Projects**. This ADB survey template provides broad coverage of project benefits, including water supply, sanitation, health, solid waste management, and flood management. It supplements the JMP core and expanded questions and the ESI survey, though they do not include flood-management

---

[5] This comprehensive set of tools used for the MICS process include overall planning, design and field data collection, data processing, analysis, interpretation, documentation, and dissemination. This tool is designed to guide survey teams, and can be obtained from the MICS website: https://mics.unicef.org/tools.

These surveys were used to develop a draft questionnaire for ADB's urban development and water supply projects, as shown in section V. The adoption of JMP core and expanded questions for data collection implies adherence to the JMP format and question wording, including the response options. However, where relevant and appropriate, modifications were made to some of the questions without changing their integrity and meaning.

The contingent valuation method (CVM) is not included in the draft questionnaire in this guidebook. This is addressed separately in the 2021 comprehensive guidebook on the CVM, by ADB's Economic Analysis and Operational Support Division (Sajise et al. 2021).

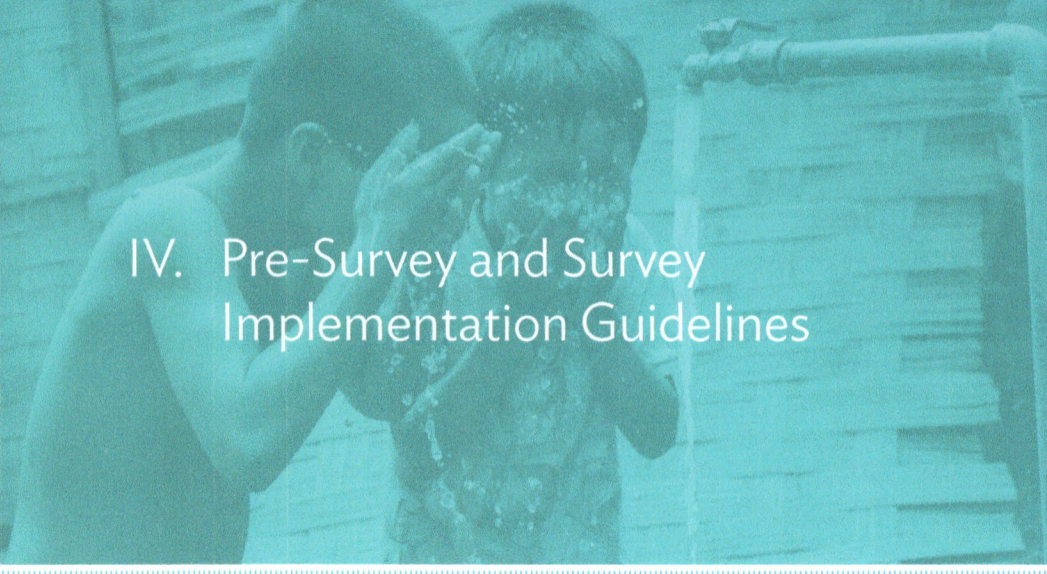

# IV. Pre-Survey and Survey Implementation Guidelines

This section discusses survey guidelines regarding ADB's best practices, particularly during the pre-survey and survey implementation stages. It is important to keep in mind that some of the activities can be done simultaneously, while others may involve a sequential process. Questionnaire development, for example, is an iterative activity that may include the collection of primary and secondary information, as well as the pretesting and refining of questions, including those based on the contingent valuation scenario.

Currently, the pandemic poses a big challenge for the implementation of ADB project surveys. While the recommendations offered in this section apply to pre-pandemic conditions, wherever possible, footnotes have been added to explain how approaches can be modified to fit the "new normal" of coronavirus disease (COVID-19)-related restrictions on site visits, personnel movement, and public gatherings.

## A. Pre-Survey Implementation Stage

### 1. Desktop Review of Other Data

Before launching into the design of a survey, a quick review of the existing data can help provide the context of the questionnaire and improve question selection, as well as assist with decisions on sampling processes.

There is always information available to draw upon. Existing data sources could include research or feasibility reports from similar projects in the area, baseline surveys, water and sanitation service assessments, large surveys such as MICS, or census data.

## 2. Conducting Key Informant Interviews and Focus Group Discussions

Key informant interviews (KIIs) are in-depth interviews with individuals such as government policy makers, local administrators, managers of water-supply and sanitation systems, and service providers who are likely to provide information, ideas, and insights into the project location and on interventions relating to urban development and water projects. It is an important field-scoping activity for gathering information that will help with the early stages of survey and questionnaire development.

In contrast to KIIs, a focus group discussion (FGD) is a semi-structured interview of people who would benefit from the intervention.[6] It often draws upon their attitudes, feelings, beliefs, experiences, and reactions regarding the project. It usually involves 10–12 participants and is facilitated by a skilled moderator for a given duration (e.g., 60–90 minutes). The goal of the moderator is to ask participants probing questions that will stimulate discussion within the group in an environment that allows them to comfortably express their thoughts and opinions (Humans of Data 2017).

The criteria for selecting FGD participants will depend on the objective of the study. In most cases, the participants are chosen based on age, gender, type of neighborhood, or social status. Groups can be homogeneous or mixed, depending on the topic being discussed. For example, some sanitation projects that deal with sensitive topics such as open defecation usually have separate FGDs for men and women. This avoids any discomfort among the participants when discussing practices that might be awkward to share in a mixed-gender group setting. Separate FGDs for men and women may also be necessary to allow women to speak freely and avoid conversations that are dominated by men.

---

[6] During the pandemic, if face-to-face FGDs are not possible, an alternative way is to conduct virtual FGDs. The researcher, however, will need to consider the target population's access to a stable internet connection, a private and quiet location, and a familiar communication platform (e.g., Google Meet, Zoom, Facebook groups). Nonetheless, if a face-to-face FGD is the only way to collect information, it must follow COVID-19 requirements such as wearing face masks and conducting the FGD in a safe environment (e.g., open space venue).

FGDs and KIIs serve as complementary data-collection tools for surveys, as well as valuable inputs for survey questionnaire design, especially for the construction of an accurate description of the contingent valuation scenario. To provide a reference for the proper design and conduct of contingent valuation studies, the Economic Analysis and Operational Support Division (EREA) published a guide in 2021 on the application of the CVM to estimate WTP.

## 3. Designing the Questionnaire

The initial step in designing a questionnaire is to decide what type of information is needed to meet the project objectives, as well as the best and most cost-effective way to gather valid and reliable information. Designers should start with the end in mind: How will the data be analyzed and used? Every question should serve a purpose, and its inclusion in the questionnaire must be justifiable and not just because it is interesting.

The questions should be designed to allow a disaggregation of the results by gender, poverty level (e.g., wealth quintiles), and other relevant socioeconomic variables where appropriate, and to help enable more in-depth economic analysis (e.g., the relationship between WTP for improved sanitation and levels of education, gender, etc). The gender questions might include the head of the household, responsibilities for water collection, the safety and risk considerations of not using a toilet at home, and decision-making regarding water and sanitation investments. Moreover, the survey questions should contribute to an understanding of the living conditions of the poorest; their access to sanitation; WTP; the barriers to, and motivations for, access to better water; and sanitation, solid-waste, and flood-management services. To support cost–benefit analysis (CBA), the questions should likewise permit the calculation of incremental and non-incremental benefits to determine the economic viability of projects.

Other important aspects of questionnaire development are addressed in section II, which offers suggestions on how to deal with common mistakes in designing questions.

## 4. Determining the Sampling Design

The sampling design must focus on the proposed beneficiaries near the project location, the purpose of the survey, and the project scope (e.g., citywide versus selected low-income settlements). To generate precise estimates, the sampling design must obtain a representative sample of the target population using stratified random sampling. The choice of the relevant stratum of the target population should allow for a reasonable representation of subgroups of special policy interest, such as different geographic areas, income groups, or status of household connections to piped water supplies (Gunatilake et al. 2007). The selected stratum must also be relevant to the outcome of the intervention. For instance, most water-supply projects classify respondent households as connected or unconnected, in order to get more complete information on respondent preferences that would help increase access to improved water supply systems.

Once the appropriate stratum has been decided upon, the sample size should be determined. The sample should be sufficiently large to enable an analysis of the results with reasonable confidence. However, it is not necessary to use very large samples since there are diminishing benefits to increasing the number of respondents. Even moderate sample sizes, if computed from an appropriate statistical formula, can represent a very large target population. If a more detailed analysis is needed for specific subpopulations—for example, to capture the WTP of poor households or the sanitation status of households headed by women—then a larger sample would be required to ensure that enough of the subpopulation is included (Ajuriagogeascoa et al. 2018).

There are various online calculators such as surveymonkey, raosoft, creative research systems, among others, that can compute the required sample sizes based on confidence level, confidence interval, and the total target population. Since the unit of analysis for ADB's urban-development and water-supply projects is households or businesses, separate samples should be drawn from each group, and they should be subject to separate analyses.

Selecting subjects to be surveyed can be done through up-to-date lists or random selections in the field. For example, a list of households connected to the piped water supply may be obtained from the database of a local water utility, while a list of unconnected households may be provided by local authorities or ward offices. A sample of respondents can then be randomly drawn from these lists. In the absence of a reliable sampling frame from which to draw a sample, new GIS-based applications can be used to randomize the selection of survey respondents within a defined survey area. This is a novel approach to the random selection of every nth household on a street or in a zone.

The sampling design needs to be properly documented, covering sample selection, sample size determination, randomization, stratification, and any issues with (or limitations of) the sampling methodology or survey process in general.

## 5. Developing a Training Manual for Enumerators

It is important to develop a good training manual for enumerators to provide them with useful reference materials during the survey training and implementation. It is best if the manual is supplemented by information on the survey design features of common methodologies used in the economic analyses, such as the CVM.

In general, a training manual may include (but is not limited to) the following information:

(i) background and objectives of the study;
(ii) survey team composition and roles;
(iii) sampling design, procedure, and data-collection schedule;
(iv) definition of terms, instructions, and notes in the survey questionnaire;
(v) the protocol and guidelines for conducting interviews (who, what, where, when, and how);
(vi) the protocol on checking, submitting, and validating questionnaires for completeness, consistency, and accuracy; and
(vii) survey visuals and metrics to be used.

## 6. Deciding on the Survey Method

There are various methods for conducting surveys, such as telephone interviews, mail surveys, face-to-face interviews, drop-off or self- administered questionnaires, and online surveys. However, the choice of survey method will depend on the type of information to be collected, the desired response rate, survey time frame, and the availability of resources, among other factors.

Due to advances in technology and the limitations imposed by the COVID-19 pandemic, online surveys and Computer-Assisted Personal Interviewing (CAPI) are gaining popularity over the traditional Pen-And-Paper Personal

Interview. CAPI is considered the better alternative because of its built-in features such as logic checks; skip patterns; geolocation ability; the ability to take photos; the ability to show videos or photographs to respondents; real-time monitoring of survey responses; and the ability to eliminate transcription errors, which are common with pen-and-paper surveys. These features make surveys more efficient, less costly, and of high quality because errors are reduced.

There are many digital survey tools available to researchers, such as mWater, Open Data Kit (ODK), KoBo Toolbox, and CommCare. These online survey platforms allow off-line data collection and can be used in remote areas with unreliable internet access. The data can be collected off-line, stored on a mobile device, and uploaded when an internet connection becomes available. Given the different features of online survey platforms, the decision on which one to use will depend on the specific data requirements of the project (e.g., cross-sectional vs longitudinal data, the need to capture global positioning system (GPS) coordinates or include videos. The familiarity of survey teams with a specific software, and the software's compatibility with national data-collection platforms and management-information systems, may also be factors to consider.

ADB is building a database of its past and ongoing projects using the KoBo Toolbox.[7] This online data-collection platform serves as host to the core and expanded questions for the urban-development and water projects of ADB. A manual for beginners provides simple and clear instructions on how to access and use the KoBo app (ADB and Egis 2020). A user's guide for KoBo Toolbox support developed by Egis (2020) provides further, detailed information on the features of the app.

CAPI allows quick modifications in the electronic questionnaire, as well as the inclusion of instructions and clarification notes after pretesting. With CAPI, it is very simple to make agreed changes in surveys and redeploy the survey instrument, so that everyone gets the latest version within seconds. This avoids the delays common with paper-based surveys when modifying questionnaires.

---

[7] The Kobo app is also linked to the Spatial Data Analysis Explorer or SPADE, which is an online platform developed by ADB in collaboration with the Royal HaskoningDHV under the Urban Climate Change Resilience Trust Fund (UCCRTF).

Another area where CAPI offers great potential is in standardizing the way in which the contingent valuation information is presented to respondents, thus avoiding enumerator bias. The contingent valuation scenario may be explained in the local dialect of the target population and illustrated through videos or photos. Presenting the scenario in a colored, three-dimensional visual form makes it more realistic, engaging, and easier for the respondents to comprehend.

To maximize the use of the CAPI technology, Brahme et. al. (2018) suggested properly selecting a mobile device and field staff who will collect the data; providing them with appropriate training and support; using concurrent reviews and feedback for monitoring; and improving data validity.

## 7. Recruiting and Training the Survey Team

To ensure the quality of the information to be gathered, enumerators, as well as field supervisors, must be carefully selected. Enumerators could be university students, public servants working in city planning offices or departments (e.g., water or sanitation), staff from nongovernment organizations (NGOs) or community-based organizations, unemployed youth, and people from the target community, among others. Ideally, survey teams should include both men and women.

Some of the criteria in choosing enumerators include survey experience, good interview skills, capacity for teamwork, familiarity with the local language, and good character. Qualification would also depend on the level of complexity of the questionnaire. The initial recruitment process may involve the submission of biodata and scheduled interviews. In some cases, preselected candidates are invited to participate in an enumerator training session where the final selection is made after their field performance is assessed by the project team.

The enumerators' training usually involves a combination of lectures, workshops, quizzes, and fieldwork. For socioeconomic surveys with a contingent valuation component, the training duration is at least 3 days, including the field trial. The training program is primarily designed to acquaint enumerators with the content, flow, structure, and organization of the questionnaire. Photocards and other visual aids are excellent visual teaching tools that help enumerators learn about the infrastructure. This is particularly important for sanitation, which can easily be miscategorized.

It is also important to clearly define the roles of the survey team members. For example, the field supervisor is tasked with managing fieldwork implementation and with making sure that the data collected are accurate, complete, and consistent. Enumerators, on the other hand, are expected to conduct high-quality interviews and follow field survey protocols. These protocols include adherence to important social customs, such as avoiding being alone with a child in the household. In some cultures, it is not also appropriate for male enumerators to interview female respondents.

Meanwhile, workshops are designed to test the enumerators' interview skills, as well as their ability to listen, observe, and record responses. An example of this is the conduct of practice interviews in the classroom by pairs of enumerators, who take turns interviewing each other. Assessment tools such as quizzes are also used to test the enumerators' understanding of concepts and questions.

Classroom lectures and workshops are complemented with supervised fieldwork. Enumerators conduct actual interviews using the draft questionnaire with at least three preselected respondents. However, in certain situations where there are security concerns or where cultural propriety is necessary (e.g., when it is inappropriate for a male to interview or be alone with a female householder), men and women are advised to work in pairs when conducting interviews. This allows female enumerators to interview female respondents. It also enables one enumerator to focus on the interview while the other observes, takes photos, or helps distract other family members.

The performance of enumerators can be evaluated in two ways. First, where electronic platforms are used, results from an in-classroom practice session can be immediately shown on screen and discussed. Fieldwork results can also be also shown afterward. Second, the project team can review, evaluate, and provide feedback on the questionnaires that were submitted or uploaded by the enumerators. The result of their overall performance may inform the final selection of enumerators for the actual survey.

As part of the questionnaire review process, the pre-pretest feedback of male and female enumerators should not be overlooked. Though they are likely to provide different feedback about wording, translation, local context etc., they can contribute to better survey design and preparation.

## 8. Conducting Pretests

Pretesting is an indispensable step in refining the content, cohesiveness, and clarity of the questionnaire before it is deployed in an actual survey. Conducting a thorough pretest could save resources and help avoid many of the problems in field survey implementation.

Pretests are typically done after the enumerators' training. The pretest subsample should include a broad representation of the main survey respondents. In contingent valuation surveys, pretests are critical for determining the accuracy of the bid levels under a dichotomous choice elicitation format.[8] Hence, it is important to have a pretest sample that is large enough (i.e., a minimum of 30 respondents per bid) to allow for a preliminary analysis of the contingent valuation data and to verify whether the bid distribution follows a downward trend. Preliminary pretest results will determine if the initial bid levels need to be adjusted for the final survey.

In general, questionnaire pretesting helps to determine if questions are properly worded and arranged, specific enough, and understandable for all classes of respondents. Respondent feedback helps to clarify, rearrange, eliminate, and simplify questions that are found to be difficult to answer.

Pretesting also benefits enumerators in several ways. First, observations of their ability to clearly articulate each question in the local dialect help to assess how well they understand the questions. Second, they help to improve the enumerators' skills in recording the collected data in CAPI; and, third, they can determine if the skip instructions given to the enumerators are correct, adequate, and easy to follow.

Another advantage of questionnaire pretesting is the use of the open-response option, which helps capture the respondents' likely answers.[9] For instance, if the respondents often select the "other, specify" option, open-ended responses that appear frequently need to be added to the list of choices. Prior knowledge of common choices will help simplify the process of data collection and analysis (FAO n.d.).

---

[8] Respondents are asked if they are willing to pay for a product or service given a certain price. The question elicits a "yes" or "no" response, similar to what respondents would give in an actual market.

[9] The open-response option is "other, specify." It allows the respondents to provide information that is not included in the question's list of options.

Lastly, it is important to emphasize that pretest results need to be properly documented, with descriptions of how the initial findings were used to improve the questionnaire.

## 9. Questionnaire Translation and Back Translation

It is important to translate the questionnaire into the local language or other ethnic minority languages of the target population in the project area. However, to ensure that the questions stay true to their original meanings and forms, the back-translation method is used. The translated version (in the local dialect) is translated back to its original version (in English).

The back translation can be done by an independent translator who has not seen the original version. The translator, however, needs to be familiar with concepts related to urban development and water supply and sanitation to ensure that translated words do not deviate from their original meaning.[10] In some languages, there are no equivalent words for concepts such as sewerage system, sanitary landfill, and recycling, so care needs to be taken regarding the translation. It may require a consensus (e.g., through a focus group discussion) to get the best translation of these terms. After the back translation is done, the two versions are then compared. Modifications may be made in the translated version, where appropriate.

There are online data apps such as mWater and KoBoToolbox that feature language options in the digital survey form that enumerators can choose from when conducting their interviews.

## B. Survey Implementation Stage
### 1. Preparing for the Survey

Survey logistics, such as the timing of the interviews, need to be planned carefully before the actual survey. Certain household members may be available only at a specific time of the day or season, and for a limited duration. It is also important for the survey team to have prior knowledge of the local culture and practices of the target population, so they can communicate effectively with the respondents. Concerns regarding the enumerators' safety and availability also need to be addressed during survey preparation.

---

[10] An independent translator who has no background in water, supply and sanitation, and hygiene (WASH) may cause more confusion (and errors) by introducing wrong terms or translating too literally (drainage and sewerage often are confused, for example).

Proper coordination with the relevant ministry or city authorities should likewise be considered at the start of the survey planning process. Sufficient time must be allotted to this activity before coordinating with the local authorities. Some countries may require a lengthier ethical approval or research review process, while others may only need a draft questionnaire to be submitted for evaluation. An endorsement letter from a local official is often given to the survey team as proof of the authority's endorsement of their activity.

The survey team should also have their identification ready, including contact numbers that the respondents can use for verification. It is also helpful if the local authorities or village leader can inform the residents in advance that a survey team will be visiting the area, and they should provide local guides to accompany the team.

## 2. Making an Introduction

There are important elements that enumerators need to remember before going ahead with a survey. First, they need to properly introduce themselves and the project, and explain the purpose of the survey. Second, they should cite the "confidentiality" clause to assure the respondents that their answers will be treated as confidential and used only for the study. Third, they must inform the respondents of the estimated duration of the survey. Finally, they need to get the respondents to agree to the survey by signing an informed consent form before proceeding with the interview. In certain instances, when the names of the respondents are randomly drawn from a list or sampling frame, they should be informed about how they were selected.

If the respondent is willing, but not available, the enumerator could come back at another time. However, if the respondent declines to be interviewed, the enumerator records the reason for the refusal, along with other information to keep track of the survey nonresponse rate. This can be done either manually through a monitoring sheet or electronically through CAPI applications.

## 3. Selecting Eligible Respondents

Household surveys often target the head of the household as respondents. The head of the household may be defined as the person considered by the household members as the main economic provider with the most authority and decision-making power on economic resources (United Nations

Department of Economics and Social Affairs 2016). The household head is often identified as male, although there can also be households headed by women with adult male members.

Household dynamics around the use of resources and decision-making can be complex, and may vary between countries and cultures. For water and sanitation, solid waste, and flooding surveys, it is not often necessary to target the head of household for an interview. Eligible respondents for socioeconomic surveys may also include the woman in the household, who is typically the water manager or caregiver. Women usually have a better overview of the household's water use, cost of water and its collection, hygiene and waste-disposal practices, and illness in the family. However, it is also acceptable for the man and woman of the household to answer the questions together.

Having defined who is eligible to participate in the survey, the enumerator needs to ascertain whether the person approached is an eligible respondent before proceeding with the interview. If the person is not an eligible respondent, the enumerator has two options: (i) end the survey and find a random replacement or (ii) set an appointment for when the eligible respondent will be available. Hence, it is important for the survey protocol to always include a replacement strategy (e.g., randomly drawn names from the target population).

## 4. Conducting the Interview

When doing in-person interviews, enumerators are advised not to interview people in groups or in the presence of nonfamily members (e.g., neighbors) because this could influence the respondents' answers. When a neighbor refuses to leave, the enumerator should inform the respondent that he or she will return for the interview at another time. It is recommended that interviews be done in private, preferably at the respondent's home. This is especially important if there are observation questions, such as those involving the inspection of water, hygiene, and sanitation facilities.[11] However, the issue of privacy needs to be qualified in the context of culture and of the safety of the respondent and enumerator, particularly for child and female respondents.

---

[11] Direct observation questions need to be reconsidered during the pandemic, especially if face-to-face interactions are not allowed. An alternative way is to rely on self-reporting by the respondents through direct questions on surveys or to ask respondents if they are willing to share pictures or videos of their water, hygiene, and sanitation facilities, using messaging apps such as Facebook Messenger.

Conducting interviews also requires good communication skills and people skills. Thus, enumerators ought to have satisfactory interviewing skills to get accurate and relevant information from the respondents.

Whittington (2002) provides some pointers for a good interview practice for enumerators in developing countries:

(i) Questions should be read exactly as written. Adhering to the precise wording of questions can shorten the interview and standardize the information provided to respondents (thereby eliciting comparable responses).

(ii) Questions must be read in a slow and clear manner in order to be understood by the respondents.

(iii) Questions should be asked once very clearly and respondents must be given time to respond. If the respondent fails to pay attention or provide an answer, the question can be repeated. If the respondent does not respond to the question the second time, the enumerator should move to the next question.

(iv) Neutrality must be maintained throughout the interview. Enumerators should refrain from expressing surprise, disapproval, judgment, or doubt in reaction to the respondent's answer. For example, if the respondent gives an answer to a knowledge question that is factually wrong, the enumerator should not show either by words or by facial expression that the answer is incorrect.

(v) Sensitive questions should be handled carefully. Enumerators need to be very matter of fact in dealing with answers to sensitive questions. They must avoid acting embarrassed, so as to avoid increasing the discomfort of respondents.

(vi) Posing suggestive questions or reading from the response options (unless there is an instruction to do so) to prompt an immediate answer from a respondent should be avoided. For example, if the respondent is having difficulty estimating his or her income or expenditures, the enumerator must not prompt him or her with suggestive question such as, *"Is your income or expenditure more than [ ] per month?"*

(vii) Providing advice or counseling to respondents on personal matters beyond the scope of the interview is discouraged. Instead, respondents should be directed to proper agencies.

(viii) Questions from respondents need clear and direct responses from the enumerators. Their questions usually revolve around the purpose of the survey, how it will be used, and how the respondents were selected for interviewing.

(ix) Careful attention to the respondent's answers is crucial in ensuring that they are properly understood and interpreted by the enumerators. Otherwise, a wrong interpretation can lead to a wrong conclusion.

## 5. Imposing Quality Control Checks during Survey Implementation

There is a need to establish protocols for survey implementation and monitoring to avoid problems that may invalidate the survey results. These problems often include missing data, wrong skipped items, and detailed questions that respondents often find difficult to answer (e.g., on income, expenditures, and the ranking of priority issues), among other problems. With the use of CAPI software, errors such as skipped questions or missing data can be avoided or drastically reduced if there are response conditions attached to those questions (i.e., use of skip logic, setting questions as mandatory or allowing a range of numerical values).

Submitted questionnaires should be subjected to closer scrutiny in terms of completeness, consistency, accuracy, and coherence before they are accepted for data encoding or processing. With thorough quality checks (whether manual or computer aided), dubious, inconsistent, outlying, or missing entries can be spotted. Field supervisors and researchers who do data checks should also be wary of response patterns for each enumerator, especially if there are too many similar responses to a question or in a section compared with what is being reported by other enumerators.

To monitor interviewer performance, the following should be noted (Gibson and Morse n.d.):

(i) **Distribution checks**. Issues that need to be examined thoroughly include the distribution of missing values and suspiciously high numbers of "I don't know" responses or refusals to answer. Another one is the frequency of "No" responses to questions with skip patterns: A question that leads to additional follow-up questions if a respondent answer "Yes" might be falsely reported by the enumerator as a "No" response, possibly to save time, cover more respondents, or make the job easier. This can be detected by comparing the number and distribution of "No" responses across enumerators.

(ii) **Outliers and inconsistent responses**. Enumerators who record a high number of outliers or inconsistent responses (e.g., reporting that a respondent does not have a toilet, but does have a septic tank) may be engaging in data fabrication or need further training. Data anomalies can be verified by the field supervisor through spot checks.

(iii) **Productivity**. Daily monitoring sheets are helpful performance indicators. They inform the field supervisor on the number of surveys completed per day, the names and locations of the people interviewed, nonresponse rates (respondents who refuse to be interviewed, and their reasons), and tracking rates (percentage of targeted respondents reached).

(iv) **Survey duration**. Extremely short interviews, as noted by the time it took to complete the interviews, can be a sign that the information was falsified.

If the project team has doubts about the integrity of how the questionnaire was administered, the field supervisor should do spot checks to validate the respondents' answers. Spot checks are unexpected visits by the field supervisor to see if the enumerators are conducting their interviews as they are supposed to. Spot checks, whether done randomly or not, should be conducted regularly for questionnaire validation. Detection of data fraud can be grounds for contract termination after the enumerator has been warned.

Another type of data check that is done in some surveys is the location audit using GPS. This allows the field supervisor to track down the interview locations to check if the enumerators are staying in one place and surveying multiple respondents. If they are, this could be a case of fraud because it would indicate that they are not following the sampling design. In addition, audio audits may also be incorporated into some survey platforms to allow the project team to listen to audio recordings. This helps verify if the enumerator is asking the questions correctly and if there are multiple speakers or none at all (Gibson and Morse n.d.).

These quality control checks are crucial because, once a completed questionnaire is submitted without thorough checking, not much can be done to correct any mistakes. Too often, resources are wasted due to the lack of proper quality monitoring and supervision at the field level.

In addition, group chat platforms (e.g., WhatsApp, Viber, Facebook Messenger, Telegram, LINE , KakaoTalk) are very useful to the field supervisor for sending messages to members of the group in real time to call back teams; arrange meetings; clarify questions, responses, and methods; share survey photos; and to keep people motivated and foster team spirit. Enumerators, supervisors, government representatives, and international consultants based outside the country can also be connected to the group.

# V. Annotated Draft Questionnaire with Core and Expanded Questions

[NOTE: This questionnaire was revised based on additional comments and suggestions from experts, including some feedback after its initial deployment on the KoBo Toolbox. For users of the draft questionnaire, the core questions are in red font, and the "skip" instructions are in blue font. The sample questionnaire is for the Philippines.]

## Introduction

Hello, I am _____. I work for _____. At the request of the Government of the _____(name of country), the Asian Development Bank (ADB) is developing a project entitled, "_____"(name of the project) in the _____(project area).

*[For the work proposed, provide a nontechnical description of the project, highlighting it's objectives and how it can benefit households as shown in the example below:*

*"The project intends to improve sanitation services and the environment by building a sewerage network to take toilet waste from homes for safe treatment and disposal. Sanitation services will be improved so as to manage the waste removed from the septic tank of households. The city authorities are also developing a plan to improve the management of toilet waste across the city."]*

Your household was randomly selected for this survey. We will greatly appreciate it if you agree to this interview; however, you can choose not to participate. Your responses will help the government plan the project, which will improve your household's *(access to water and sanitation facilities and services)*.

# Annotated Draft Questionnaire with Core and Expanded Questions

We would like to assure you that any information you provide will be recorded anonymously and treated as confidential. Should you choose to participate, please remember that there are no right or wrong answers. We would only like to get your honest opinions. It will probably take about ( ) minutes to complete the survey. In case you need more information about the project, you may contact the person listed on this card. [Give card with contact information.] Thank you.

## Screener questions:

- Are you the head of the household or an eligible person for the interview (e.g., household water manager, caregiver)?
  [Note: The head of the household is an adult person, male or female, who can either be the breadwinner, the main decision-maker, the oldest person in the family, or who is regarded as the head by the other members of the household. These norms may vary across countries, within countries, or across income groups].

  0 – No [Stop the interview]
  1 – Yes

- [If yes] Do you have any questions before we start the interview?
  0 – None
  1 – Yes [Enumerator addresses the questions]

- If you have no more questions, may I begin the interview now?
  0 – No, refuses to participate [Stop the interview and ask the reason for refusal]
  1 – Yes [Ask to sign a consent form, then proceed with the interview.]

Screener questions are administered prior to the survey proper. They prevent enumerators from interviewing non-eligible respondents, and they secure the consent of eligible respondents for their interviews.

If the questionnaire is designed to be answered by the eligible member of the household (as defined by the project), enumerators should make sure that they are interviewing the eligible respondent.

If the eligible person is not available, the enumerator can come back at a set time when he or she will be available.

It is also important to ask the respondents for any questions or clarifications they may have before proceeding with the interview. The enumerator should politely respond to these questions the best way he or she can, or refer the respondents to the field supervisor for guidance.

The enumerator should then politely ask for the respondent's consent to begin the interview before proceeding with the questions. Consent should be written, not just oral.

> **Insert Socioeconomic Questions:**
>
> [Note: Each country can include relevant sociodemographic variables that they intend to use for subgroup analysis.]
>
> At the minimum, relevant sociodemographic variables may include:
> - Age of the head of household (i.e., the respondent)
> - Gender of the head of household
> - Highest level of education of the head of household
> - Household income [may be asked last]
> - Household size
> - Ownership of buildings and/or land
> - House characteristics (electricity connection; construction materials of the roof, walls, floors, etc.)
> - Wealth quintile and asset questions (country specific, urban–rural variations)
>
> Optional
> - Question on disabilities (Washington Group questions on disabilities)

## Section 1: Water Supply and Use

### Water Service Providers

H1. Is your household connected to a piped water network?
  1. Yes   [Skip to H3]
  2. No

*This subsection provides information on the respondent's piped water supply if they are connected to one (H1 is a screener question).*

H2. [If no] Why is your household not connected? [Single response]
  1. Water supply system unavailable in our area  [Skip to H19]
  2. Expensive connection fees  [Skip to H19]
  3. Expensive water user fees  [Skip to H19]
  4. Bad quality of drinking water  [Skip to H19]
  5. Poor service quality  [Skip to H19]
  6. Other (specify)  [Skip to H19]

H3. Is your piped water connection metered?
1. Yes
2. No

*Questions H3–H5 cover some basic information on the characteristics of the respondent's piped water connection, including the existence of a meter, length of the connection, and who manages the piped water system.*

H4. How long has your household had a piped water connection?
No. of years_____[integer]
Don't know_____998

H5. Who manages your piped water supply system?
1. Private water service provider
2. Public water service provider
3. Community-based water users' group or association
4. Other (specify)

H6. How much did you pay for the connection fee?
₱ (pesos)_____[integer]
Don't know_____998

*Questions H6–H13 address the cost of connecting to the piped water supply, which includes the connection fee, subsidy (if any), construction materials purchased, the hired labor, and the opportunity cost of the time spent by family members.*

H7. How was the connection fee paid?
1. Lump sum
2. Installment
3. Free (no payment)

H8. Did you qualify for a subsidy?
1. Yes, a full subsidy (free)
2. Yes, a partial subsidy
3. No, paid the connection fee in full [Skip to H10]

H9. [If qualified for a subsidy] How much was the subsidy for the water connection fee?
₱(pesos)_____[integer]
Don't know_____998

H10. To connect to the piped water network, did you have to purchase any pipes or other construction materials, or did you have to pay for the labor?
1. Yes
2. No [Skip to H12]

H11. How much did you spend for the pipes, other construction materials, and labor?
₱(pesos)_____[integer]
Don't know_____998

H12. Did any of your family members provide labor as part of your contribution for your household's pipe water connection?
 1. Yes
 2. No [Skip to H14]

H13. [If yes], how many hours in total were spent by all household members in order to connect to the piped water system?
No of hours_____[integer]
Don't know_____998

H14. How many hours per day is piped water supplied on average?
 1. 24 hours per day
 2. 18–24 hours per day
 3. 12–17 hours per day
 4. 6–11 hours per day
 5. <6 hours per day
 6. Don't know

**Questions H14–H18** focus on the current situation of the piped water supply in terms of:

water availability (H14–H15)
water reliability (H16–H17)
water quality (H18)
Other water service attributes (H18)

These responses can be used as individual variables or as an index for the contingent valuation method (CVM).

H15. How many days per week is piped water supplied on average?
No. of days/week_____[integer]
Don't know_____998

H16. In the past 12 months, has your piped water supply ever been ever cut off for a day or more?
 1. Yes, several times
 2. Yes, a few times
 3. Yes, once
 4. No [Skip to H18]

H17. [If yes], How long were these breakdowns on average?
No of days_____[integer]
Don't know_____998

H18. From a scale of 1–5 (5 being the highest), how would you rate the quality of your piped water and the water-related services? [Write 999 if the response is "not applicable" or if the respondent did not experience any repairs or make any complaints to the water service provider.]

| Attributes | Very poor | Poor | Neutral | Good | Very good |
|---|---|---|---|---|---|
| Clarity (clear and colorless) of the water | 1 | 2 | 3 | 4 | 5 |
| Smell of the water | 1 | 2 | 3 | 4 | 5 |
| Taste of the water | 1 | 2 | 3 | 4 | 5 |
| Water pressure | 1 | 2 | 3 | 4 | 5 |
| Reliability of water meter | 1 | 2 | 3 | 4 | 5 |
| Regularity of billing and collection | 1 | 2 | 3 | 4 | 5 |
| Accuracy (correctness) of the billing | 1 | 2 | 3 | 4 | 5 |
| Responsiveness to customer complaints | 1 | 2 | 3 | 4 | 5 |
| Repair time and service | 1 | 2 | 3 | 4 | 5 |

## Water Sources and Use

H19. What is the main source of drinking water for members of your household? [Single response]
   1. Water piped into dwelling [Skip to H25]
   2. Water piped into compound, yard, or plot [Skip to H25]
   3. Water piped to neighbor
   4. Public tap or standpipe
   5. Tube well or borehole
   6. Protected well
   7. Unprotected well
   8. Protected spring
   9. Unprotected spring
   10. Collected rainwater
   11. Tanker truck
   12. Cart with small tank or drum
   13. Water kiosk
   14. Bottled water or purified water
   15. Sachet water
   16. Anytime Water Machine (ATM) or automated water-dispensing unit
   17. Surface water (from a river, stream, dam, lake, pond, canal, or irrigation channel)
   18. Other (specify)

H20. Who manages your drinking water supply? [Write 999 if the drinking water supply is piped to household dwelling, compound, yard, or plot]
1. Private water service provider
2. Public water service provider
3. Community-based water user's group or association
4. Individual households
5. Other (specify)

H21. Where is the main source of drinking water located?
1. In the respondent's own dwelling
2. In the respondent's own yard or plot
3. Elsewhere

H22. How long does it usually take to go there, get the water, and come back? [Record the total time taken for a single round trip, including waiting in line and filling the water containers.]
No. of minutes (per round trip)_____[integer]
Don't know _____998
Source is on the premises_____999
Water is delivered_____999

*Questions H22 and H23 enable the computation of the total time spent collecting drinking water from the primary source outside the house. This translates into the time saved by households after shifting to a piped water supply.*

H23. How many trips to the source does a member of your household usually make per week?
No. of round trips/week_____[integer]
Don't know_____998
Source is on premises_____999
Water is delivered_____999

H24. Who usually goes to the main drinking source to fetch water for your household? [Single response.]
1. Adult woman (> 15 years)
2. Adult man (> 15 years)
3. Female child (≤ 15 years)
4. Male child (≤ 15 years)

H25. What is the main source of water used by your household for other purposes, such as handwashing?

**Question H25** is the main source of water used by the household for other purposes

1. Water piped into dwelling [Skip to H29]
2. Water piped into dwelling, yard, or plot [Skip to H29]
3. Water piped to neighbor
4. Public tap or standpipe
5. Tube well or borehole
6. Protected well
7. Unprotected well
8. Protected spring
9. Unprotected spring
10. Collected rainwater
11. Tanker truck
12. Cart with small tank or drum
13. Water kiosk
14. Bottled or purified water
15. Sachet water
16. Anytime Water Machine (ATM) or automated water-dispensing unit
17. Surface water (from a river, stream, dam, lake, pond, canal, or irrigation channel)
18. Other (specify)

H26. How long does it usually take to go there, get the water, and come back? [Record the total time taken for a single round trip, including waiting in line and filling the water containers.]

The time spent accessing the main water source outside the home to get water for other purposes, such as cooking and handwashing, can be computed from **questions H26 and H27**.

Note: Additional time savings from H26–H27 should only be included if the response to H25 (water used for other purposes) is different from that to H19 (main source of drinking water).

No. of minutes (per round trip) _____ [integer]
Don't know _____ 998
Source is on the premises _____ 999
Water is delivered _____ 999

H27. How many trips did that person make in the last week?
    No. of round trips per week_____[integer]
    Don't know                         _____998
    Source is on the premises_____999
    Water is delivered_____999

H28. Who usually goes to the main source for other uses such as cooking and handwashing, to fetch water for your household? [Single response.]
    1. Adult woman (> 15 years)
    2. Adult man (> 15 years
    3. Female child (≤ 15 years)
    4. Male child (≤ 15 years)

**Water Availability**

H29. Is water always available from your main source of drinking water?
    1. Yes, water is always available
    2. No, water is available most of the time
    3. No, water is available some of the time
    4. No, water is rarely available
    5. Don't know

*This subsection looks at the availability and sufficiency of water supplies from the main drinking source, including the constraints on water access (H29–H40).*

H30. In the past month, have there been any times when your household did not have sufficient quantities of drinking water when needed?
    1. Yes, at least once
    2. No, the quantity is always sufficient  [Skip to H33]
    3. Don't know [Skip to H33]

H31. [If yes] What was the main reason you were unable to access sufficient quantities of water when needed? [Single response]
    1. Water was not available from the source
    2. Water was too expensive
    3. The source was not accessible
    4. Other (specify)

H32. In the past month, for how many hours was water from your main source of drinking water unavailable when needed?
    No. of hours_____[integer]
    Don't know_____998
    Water was always available_____999

H33. Does your household have a large storage tank?
1. Yes
2. No [Skip to H39]

**Questions H33–H40** examine the water-storage practices of households, that is to say, their coping strategies when water was inadequate or unavailable. Storing water is a way for households to secure their supplies in case of a water shortage.

H34. [If yes] How many liters does the storage tank hold?
No. of liters_____[integer]
Don't know_____998

H35. How many times has the storage tank been filled in the past week or in the past month?
No. of times per week_____[integer]
No. of times per month_____[integer]
Don't know_____998

H36. Have you maintained (e.g., inspected, cleaned, and disinfected) your storage tank over the past 12 months?
1. Yes
2. No [Skip to H39]

H37. [If yes] Did you pay for the maintenance of your storage tank in the past 12 months?
1. Yes
2. No [Skip to H39]

H38. [If yes] How much did you spend in the past 12 months for the maintenance of your storage tank?
₱pesos)_____[integer]
Don't know_____998

**Question H38**, regarding the household's expenditures on storage-tank maintenance, can be viewed as a measurement of the benefit (expenditure saved) when the availability and reliability of water supplies are improved through the proposed water supply project.

H39. Has there been any time in the past month when you have not been able to store sufficient water to meet your needs?
1. Yes, at least once
2. No
3. Don't know

H40. Does your household store drinking water in small containers? [Single response] [Ask the respondent if you can see the storage containers.]
  1. Water is not stored in small containers
  2. Water is stored in small covered containers
  3. Water is stored in small uncovered containers
  4. Unable to observe

**Water Quality**

H41. Is the water supplied from your main drinking source usually acceptable? If it usually unacceptable, select the main reason. [Single response]
  1. Yes, acceptable
  2. No, unacceptable taste
  3. No, unacceptable color
  4. No, unacceptable smell
  5. No, contains materials
  6. No, other reason (specify)

*The questions in this subsection deal with water quality as an important attribute of a drinking water source. It looks primarily at the household's coping strategy when the water quality is poor. This is evident in the household's water-treatment practices.*

H42. Have you or any other household members done anything to your water to make it safer to drink?
  1. Yes
  2. No [Skip to H50]

H43. [If yes] What do you usually do to the water to make it safer to drink? [Multiple responses]

| | | | |
|---|---|---|---|
| Boil it | 1 (Yes) | 2 (No) | [If no] Skip to H50 |
| Add bleach or chlorine | 1 (Yes) | 2 (No) | Skip to H48 |
| Strain it through a cloth | 1 (Yes) | 2 (No) | |
| Use a water filter (ceramic, sand, composite, reverse osmosis, etc.) | 1 (Yes) | 2 (No) | |
| Use solar disinfection | 1 (Yes) | 2 (No) | |
| Let it stand and settle | 1 (Yes) | 2 (No) | |
| Other (specify) | 1 (Yes) | 2 (No) | |
| Don't know | 1 (Yes) | 2 (No) | |

H44. Which source of energy do you mostly use for boiling?
[Single response]
1. Electricity [Skip to H48]
2. Charcoal
3. Firewood
4. Liquid gas or kerosene [Skip to H48]
5. Other (specify) [Skip to H48]

H45. [If the household uses wood or charcoal] How does your household obtain the fuel?
1. Fuel is purchased [Skip to H48]
2. Fuel is collected by household members
3. Fuel is obtained through other means [Skip to H48]

H46. [If the fuel is collected by household members] How often is this done per week?
No. of times per week_____[integer]
Don't know _____998 [Skip to H48]
Fuel is collected sometimes or rarely _____999 [Skip to H48]

H47. How much time do household members usually spend collecting wood or charcoal for all purposes (cooking, boiling water for drinking, etc.)?
[Record the total time taken for a single round trip]
No. of minutes/week_____[integer]
Don't know_____998

H48. If you treat your drinking water [refer to H43], how much does your household spend per month on any of the following treatments? [Write "999" if the household does not treat its water using these methods]

**H48–H49** address the additional expenditures households incur by treating their water using the methods listed. The avoidance of these costs would be considered a benefit, in the form of "expenditure savings," if the water quality were improved through the proposed water supply project.

| | |
|---|---|
| Filters (disposable filters, cloth, or other strainers) | ₱/month |
| Sterilizing tablets (bleach or chlorine) | ₱/month |
| Aluminum sulphate treatments | ₱/month |
| Other treatment (specify) | ₱/month |

H49. If your household owns a water-filtering system [refer to H43], what was its purchase price?
₱(pesos)_____[integer]
Don't know _____998

## Water Expenditures

H50. How much does the household usually spend on water per month for piped water and water from all other sources (including the tariff, water collection or delivery fees, and transport cost)? [Refer to H19 and H25 for the main sources of water used. Write 998 if respondent cannot estimate the water expenditure]

**H50** is a straightforward question regarding the household's total monthly expenditure for water from all sources. The avoidance of these costs would be considered a benefit, in the form of expenditure savings, if the household were to shift to a piped water supply, given the improvements expected from the proposed water supply intervention.

| Water source | Total ependiture/month |
| --- | --- |
| Piped water | ₱ (pesos)/month |
| All other water sources | ₱ (pesos)/month |

[Insert contingent valuation module on the household's willingness to pay for improved water supply services.]

## Section 2: Sanitation Services

### On-site sanitation facilities

H51. What kind of toilet facility do the members of your household usually use? If it is a 'flush' or 'pour' toilet facility, where does it flush to? [Single response]

*Questions H51–H61 primarily look at the household's toilet facility and its characteristics—whether it is shared, accessible, private, and environmentally safe.*

1. Flush or pour, flushes into piped sewer system
2. Flush or pour, flushes into septic tank
3. Flush or pour, flushes into pit latrine
4. Flush or pour, flushes into open drain
5. Flush or pour, flushes into unknown receptacle
6. Dry pit latrine with slab
7. Dry pit latrine without slab or an open pit
8. Composting toilet- Twin pits with slab
9. Composting toilet- Twin pits without slab
10. Other type of composting toilet
11. Bucket
11. Container-based sanitation
12. Hanging toilet or hanging latrine
13. No toilet facility, instead use of bushes or field [Skip to H70]
14. Other (specify)

H52. Do you share this facility with others who are not members of your household?
1. Yes
2. No [Skip to H54]

H53. [If yes] How many households in total use this toilet facility, including your own household?
No. of households_____[integer]
Don't know_____998

H54. Where is this toilet facility located? [Single response]
1. In own dwelling
2. In own yard or plot
3. Elsewhere

H55. Are there any safety risks for women or girls when they use the toilet? [Single response. Risks include being attacked, assaulted, or harassed]
1. No risks faced
2. Yes, some risks
3. Very unsafe

H56. Does the design of your toilet prevent other people from seeing and hearing what you are doing when you use it?
1. Yes
2. No

H57. Do all the household members use the sanitation facility?
1. Yes [Skip to H59]
2. No

H58. [If no], who among the household members is not using the toilet facility?

| Name of household member | Gender | Age |
|---|---|---|
|  |  |  |

H59. The last time the youngest child in the family defecated, what was done to dispose of the stools? [Single response]
1. Child used the toilet or latrine
2. Rinsed away in toilet or latrine
3. Rinsed away in drain or ditch
4. Thrown into the garbage (solid waste)
5. Buried
6. Left out in the open
7. Used as manure
8. Other (specify)
9. Don't know

H60. Is everyone in the household able to access and use the toilet at all times of the day and night?
1. Yes [Skip to H62]
2. No

H61. [If no] What was the main reason why household members were unable to use the toilet at any time of the day or night? [Single response]
1. Limited mobility prevents members from using the toilet
2. Distance or barriers prevent members from reaching the toilet
3. Toilet is not always available to all household members
4. Toilet is not always safe for all household members to use
5. Other (specify)

H62. Does your sanitation facility leak or overflow with waste at any time of year, such as during the rainy season or floods? [Single response]
1. No, never
2. Yes, sometimes
3. Yes, frequently
4. Don't know

H63. What type of anal cleansing material is most commonly used by members of this household? ["Anal cleansing material" refers to what is used for wiping after defecating]
1. Toilet tissue paper
2. Newspaper
3. Other paper (e.g., school notebook paper)
4. Water only
5. Water and soap
6. Cardboard
7. Cloth, old rags
8. Stones
9. Leaves, grasses
10. Sticks
11. Nothing
12. Other (specify)

H64. Do you use or sold feces as fertilizer?
1. Yes, use as fertilizer
2. Yes, sold as fertilizer [Skip to H66]
3. No [Skip to H67 if the current toilet facility indicated in H51 is a bucket or composting unit. If the current toilet facility is neither, and does not include a septic tank or pit latrine, skip to H83. Otherwise, skip to H90.]

**H64** pertain to households that reuse the feces as fertilizer for plants and/or farm products, or that sell them as fertilizer.

H65. If feces are used as fertilizer for plants and/or farm products, how much has this saved you in fertilizer costs over the last 12 months?
₱(pesos)/year_____
[integer]
Don't know_____998

**Questions H65 and H66** measure benefits such as the amount of fertilizer saved by using human waste or the income earned from selling feces as fertilizer.

[Skip to H67 if the current toilet facility indicated in H51 is a bucket or composting unit. If the current toilet facility is neither, and does not include a septic tank or pit latrine, skip to H83. Otherwise, skip to H90]

H66. If the feces are sold as fertilizer, how much did you earn over the past 12 months?
₱/year_____[integer]
Don't know_____998

[Skip to H67 if the current toilet facility indicated in H51 is a bucket or composting unit. If the current toilet facility is neither, and does not include a septic tank or pit latrine, skip to H83. Otherwise, skip to H90.]

H67. [For households using a bucket or composting toilet] Do you have enough sources of ash or other materials (e.g. sawdust) to cover the feces?
1. Yes
2. No

**Questions H67–H68** concern the use of ash and other materials (e.g., sawdust) to cover the feces in buckets and composting toilets. Question H69 measures the costs incurred by households in securing ash or other materials (e.g., sawdust). The avoidance of the costs of ash or other materials would be considered a benefit, in the form of expenditure savings, if the households built an improved toilet facility.

H68. How do you usually get the ash or other materials (e.g. sawdust)?
1. Collected [Skip to H83]
2. Bought
3. Given [Skip to H83]
4. Others (specify) [Skip to H83]

H69. If the ash or other materials (e.g. sawdust) are bought, how much do you spend per month?
₱ (pesos)/month_____[integer] [Skip to H83]
Don't know_____998 [Skip to H83]

[If the household has no toilet facilities, resume questioning here]

H70. Where do you and the other adult household members usually go to defecate? ? [Single response]
1. Designated place in the yard
2. Neighbors' or relatives' toilet (shared)
3. Public toilet
4. Designated area on nearby community or other public land
5. By the river, lake, pond, or canal
6. To bushes or a forest
7. Other (specify)

**H70–H82** are questions for those who do not have a toilet facility. These group are also considered as open defecators.

H71. How long does it usually take you to go there and come back? [Record the total time taken for a single round trip to the defecation area]
No. of minutes (per round trip)
_____[integer]
Don't know_____998

**Questions H71–H76** refer to the respondent's answer to H70 on where households without toilets usually go to defecate. It provides information on the travel time, waiting time, and privacy, as well as the safety risks of going to the defecation area.

**Question H71** measures the time savings per trip to the defecation spot if the household were to have its own toilet facility.

H72. Do you sometimes have to wait to have privacy before you can defecate?
1. Yes
2. No [Skip to H74]

H73. [If yes] How often do you have to wait?
1. Always
2. Often
3. Sometimes
4. Rarely
5. Don't know

H74. During the times you have to wait, how long do you usually end up waiting?
No. of minutes_____[integer]
Don't know_____998

H75. Are there any safety risks for women and girls when they use the defecation area? [Risks include being attacked, assaulted, or harassed]
1. No risks faced
2. Yes, some risks
3. Very unsafe

**Questions H75–H76** concerns the safety of women and girls, especially when they use an outdoor space (bushes, field, etc.). This is an important factor in a household's decision to build a toilet of its own.

H76. Do women and girls have privacy when they use the defecation area?
1. Yes
2. No

H77. If your household uses public toilets [refer to H70], do you have to pay a fee? [Payment could be per use, family subscription per week, etc.]
1. Yes
2. No [Skip to H79]

**Questions H77–H78** measure the total monthly household expenditure for the use of public toilets that charge a fee (per use, per week, etc.). The avoidance of this fee could be considered a benefit if a household were to have its own toilet facility.

H78. [If yes] How much does your household usually spend per month to use the public toilet?
₱ (pesos) per month _____ [integer]
Don't know_____ 998

H79. Are you willing to construct your own toilet facility?
1. Yes [Skip to H81]
2. No

**Questions H79–H82** concern a household's willingness to build its own toilet facility, taking into account the difficulties involved in building one.

H80. [If no] What is the main reason? [Single response]
1. Too expensive, we cannot afford the cost [Skip to H88]
2. No space in the yard to build one [Skip to H88]
3. Do not own the lot and/or the house [Skip to H88]
4. Prefer existing toilet arrangements [Skip to H88]
5. Not enough water available [Skip to H88]
6. Other (specify) [Skip to H88]

H81. [If yes] When do you plan to build one?
1. Within the next 6 months
2. In the next 6 months to one year
3. After 1 year to 2 years
4. After two years
5. Don't know

H82. [If yes] How much do you think it will cost you?  
₱(pesos)_____  
[integer] [Skip to H88]  
Don't know_____ 998 [Skip to H88]

*In response to **question H82**, the respondents are expected to estimate the cost of building a toilet, depending on the type of facility they prefer.*

## Septic Facilities

[If the current toilet facility, as defined by the response to question H51, does not have a septic tank or pit latrine, proceed to questions H83–H89. For toilet facilities with a septic tank or pit latrine, skip to H90.]

H83. If your household does not have a [pit latrine or septic tank], why not? [Single response]
1. Do not know what a septic tank is
2. Too expensive, we cannot afford the cost
3. No space in the yard to build one
4. We don't own the lot and/or house
5. Prefer existing toilet arrangements
6. Not enough water available
7. Other (specify)

H84 Would you be willing to construct a septic tank?
1. Yes [Skip to H86]
2. No
3. Don't know [Skip to H86]

*Questions **H84–H87** gauge the willingness of households without a septic tank to build one, taking into account the difficulties they would face.*

H85. [If no] What are the reasons? [Multiple response]

| Too expensive, we cannot afford the cost | 1 (Yes) | 2 (No) | After receiving a response, skip to H88. |
| No space in the yard to build one | 1 (Yes) | 2 (No) | |
| We don't own the lot and/or house | 1 (Yes) | 2 (No) | |
| Other (specify) | 1 (Yes) | 2 (No) | |

H86. [If yes] When do you plan to build your septic tank?
   1. In less than 6 months
   2. From 6 months to 1 year
   3. After 1 year to 2 years
   4. After 2 years
   5. Don't know

H87. [If yes] How much do you think will this cost you?
   ₱(pesos)_____[integer]
   Don't know_____998

In addition, **Question H87** asks those who want to build a septic tank how much they intend to spend. The amount they suggest will more or less reflect what they can afford to pay.

**H88–H89** ask households without a toilet or septic tank if they would be willing to borrow money to build one. This is especially important for those households that identify affordability as their main constraint in their responses to H80 and H85.

H88. If credit were available to you on preferential terms (affordable repayment, no collateral, etc.) for building a toilet facility or septic tank, would your family be willing to borrow the money?
   1. Yes
   2. No [Skip to H104]

H89. How much could you afford to pay back per month for a sanitation loan?
   ₱(pesos)_____[integer] [Skip to H104]
   Don't know_____998 [Skip to H104]

## Households with a Septic Tank or Pit Latrine

This subsection is for households with a septic tank or pit latrine. The questions address some important characteristics of the containment facility, such as where the waste is discharged; the facility's age, location, and accessibility for desludging; and the cost of construction (**H90–H95**).

H90. What does your [pit latrine or septic tank] discharge into?
 1. Leach field or soakaway pit
 2. Sewer
 3. Open drain
 4. Open ground or watercourse
 5. Don't know
 6. Other (specify)

H91. How many years ago was your [pit latrine or septic tank] built?
 No. of year_____[integer]
 Don't know_____998

H92. Where is the [pit latrine or septic tank] located?
 1. Inside the house
 2. Outside the house
 3. Other (specify)

H93. Is your house accessible for [pit latrine or septic tank] emptying by a vacuum tanker?
 1. Yes
 2. No
 3. Don't know_____998

H94. Is the [pit latrine or septic tank] accessible for fecal sludge removal?
 1. No, it is necessary to break the slab
 2. No, it is necessary to remove the toilet squat
 3. Yes, it is accessible by an access hatch or a hole (only with a pipe)
 4. Don't know
 5. Other (specify)

H95. How much was the cost of building the [pit latrine or septic tank]?
 ₱(pesos)_____[integer]
 Don't know_____998

H96. Did your [pit latrine or septic tank] undergo any repairs during the past 12 months?
1. Yes
2. No [Skip to H98]

H97. [If yes] How much did the repairs cost?
₱(pesos)_____[integer]
Don't know_____998

H98. Has your [pit latrine or septic tank] ever been emptied?
1. Yes
2. No [Skip to the CV module on improved septic services]
3. Don't know [Skip to the CV module on improved septic services]

**Questions H96–H104** provide information on the repair and maintenance of the household's containment facility. They also collect other information, such as whether the containment facility has ever been emptied, why it was emptied, when it was last emptied, who emptied it, and where the contents were disposed of.

In addition, **questions H97 and H104** ask the households about their spending on pit latrine or septic tank repair and maintenance, particularly for emptying and desludging. The avoidance of these costs would be a benefit, in the form of expenditure savings, if the household's toilet facility were directly connected to the sewer lines.

H99. [If yes] When was your [pit latrine or septic tank] last emptied?
Within the last 12 months_____000
Years ago_____[integer]
Don't know           _____998

H100. [If yes] Why did you empty your [pit latrine or septic tank]?
1. [Pit latrine or septic tank] full, though not overflowing
2. [Pit latrine or septic tank] overflowing or toilet clogged
3. Bad odor
4. Complaints from neighbors
5. Action imposed by the hygiene authorities
6. Response to an awareness or communication campaign
7. Regular maintenance
8. Other (specify)

H101. When your [pit latrine or septic tank] was last emptied, who emptied it?
1. Mechanical service provider (e.g., vacuum truck)
2. Manual service provider
3. The household [Skip to H103]
4. Other (specify) [Skip to H103]

H102. What type of operator was the service provider?
1. Private company
2. Public company
3. Don't know

H103. The last time you emptied your [pit latrine or septic tank], how much did you spend?
₱(pesos)_____[integer]
Don't know_____998

> Insert the contingent valuation module on the household's willingness to pay for improved septic services.

## Sewerage System

*This subsection focuses on the questions of how wastewater is currently disposed of and if there is a sewerage system in the area.*

H104. How do you dispose of household water that has been used for cooking, laundry, and bathing?
1. Sink or drain connected to a sewer
2. Sink or drain connected to a septic tank
3. Sink or drain connected to a pit
4. Sink or drain connected to a soakaway pit
5. Sink or drain connected to open drain or open ground
6. Disposal directly into open ground or a body of water
7. Not applicable (cooking, laundry, and bathing are done outside the household)
8. Don't know

H105. Is there a sewerage system in your area?
1. Yes
2. No [Skip to H114]
3. Don't know [Skip to H114]

H106. [If yes] Are you connected to the sewerage system?
1. Yes [Skip to H108]
2. No

*Questions H106–H113 explore the household's decision to connect to the local sewerage system, taking into account the constraints involved.*

H107. [If no] What is the main reason why you not connected? [Single response]
1. Connection fee too expensive
2. Service fee too expensive
3. Cost of changing plumbing arrangements too expensive
4. Inadequate information
5. Prefer existing wastewater disposal method
6. Other (specify)
[Skip to the CV module on improved sewerage services.]

H108. If currently connected to a sewerage system, how much was the connection fee?
₱ (pesos)_____[integer]
Don't know_____998

H109. Did you have to purchase any pipes or other construction materials, or pay for labor in order to connect to the sewerage network?
1. Yes
2. No [Skip to H111]

**Questions H108–H113** establish the cost of connecting to the local sewerage system. This includes the connection fee, the additional pipes and other construction materials that households need to purchase, the cost of hired labor, and the opportunity cost for family members contributing their labor. As with piped water, the high cost of a sewerage-system connection may serve as a strong deterrent for households when they are deciding whether to connect to the sewerage system. H113 directly asks the monthly sewerage fee that households must pay.

H110. [If yes] How much did you spend in total for the pipes, other construction materials, and labor?
₱ (pesos)_____ [integer]
Don't know_____998

H111. Did any of your family members provide labor as a contribution to your household's sewerage connection?
1. Yes
2. No [Skip to H113]

H112 [If yes] How many total hours of work were contributed by household members?
No. of hours_____[integer]
Don't know_____998

H113. How much are you currently paying per month for your sewerage service?
₱ (pesos)_____[integer]
Don't know_____998

> Insert the contingent valuation module on the household's willingness to pay for improved sewerage services.

## Section 3: Solid Waste Management

H114. How does your household usually dispose of its garbage? [Single response]
1. Collected by a formal service provider
2. Collected by an informal service provider
3. Dropped off at a designated waste-disposal area, from where it is collected by a formal or informal service provider
4. Disposed of within the household yard or plot
5. Buried or burned
6. Disposed of elsewhere
7. Don't know

*This section includes questions on household behavior, particularly how the household manages its garbage (e.g., whether it segregates the organic food waste and engages in proper garbage-disposal practices).*

*It also explores the current solid waste services available to the household (H114–H122), such as the service provider, frequency of garbage collection, and the monthly fee. H122 looks at the household's level of satisfaction with the solid-waste management services in terms of frequency, collection time, garbage fee, and the cleanliness of the area after collection. This may influence a household's willingness to pay for the improved solid-waste management services that will be provided by the project.*

H115. Do you dispose of organic food waste separately from inorganic materials?
1. Yes
2. No [Skip to H117]

H116. [If yes] How do you dispose of your organic waste?
1. Composted
2. Given to animals as feed
3. Thrown into an open space
4. Thrown into the backyard
5. Given to an informal collector
6. Other (specify)

H117. Does the household sell items to informal buyers (e.g., cans, metal, paper, etc)?
1. Yes
2. No

H118. If garbage is collected by a formal service provider [refer to H114], who provides the service?
1. Private company
2. Public company
3. I don't know

H119. How often is the waste collected per week? [Single response]
1. More than once a day
2. Once a day
3. Every 2 days
4. Every 3 days
5. Every 4 days
6. Every 5 days
7. Once a week
8. I don't know

H120. Do you pay any monthly fee for garbage collection?
1. Yes
2. No [Skip to H122]

H121 How much do you pay monthly for garbage collection?
1. ₱(pesos) per month_____[integer]
2. Don't know_____998

H122. From a scale of 1–5 (5 being the highest), how satisfied are you with the current state of solid waste collection in your area?
[Single response per row]

|  | Very dissatisfied | Dissatisfied | Neither dissatisfied not satisfied | Satisfied | Very Satisfied |
| --- | --- | --- | --- | --- | --- |
| Frequency of collection | 1 | 2 | 3 | 4 | 5 |
| Time of garbage collection | 1 | 2 | 3 | 4 | 5 |
| Garbage fee | 1 | 2 | 3 | 4 | 5 |
| Cleanliness of the area after collection | 1 | 2 | 3 | 4 | 5 |
| Overall satisfaction | 1 | 2 | 3 | 4 | 5 |

Insert the contingent valuation module on the household's willingness to pay for improved solid waste management.

## Section 4: Health and Hygiene

H123. Where do you and other members of your household most often wash your hands?
1. Sink or tap in dwelling
2. Sink or tap in the yard or on the plot
3. Mobile object (e.g., bucket, jug, or kettle)
4. No handwashing place in the dwelling, yard, or on the plot
5. No permission to see
6. Other (specify)

For hygiene, only the core questions from the WHO/UNICEF Joint Monitoring Programme for Water Supply, Sanitation and Hygiene (JMP) are included. **Questions H124 and H125** require observation. The enumerator needs to get the consent of the respondent to check the handwashing area for the presence of soap and water. This means that the survey should be conducted at the respondent's home.

**Questions H129–138** cover the health impacts of poor water and sanitation, though it is often very difficult to separate the health impacts of these factors.

In addition, **Questions H126–H128** focus mainly on children under 5 years of age because this is a very vulnerable population in terms of mortality cases.

H124. Observe the availability of water at the place for handwashing. [Verify by checking the tap or pump, or the basin, bucket, water container, or similar objects for presence of water.]
1. Water is available
2. Water is not available

H125. Observe the availability of soap or detergent at the place for handwashing.
1. Soap is available
2. Soap is not available

H126. In the last two weeks, has any child under 5 years of age in your household had diarrhea? [Diarrhea is indicated when there are three or more loose or watery stools in a day.]

[Write 999 if: (i) there is no child under 5 in the household; and (ii) no child under 5 had diarrhea.] [Skip to H129]

| Age (in years and months) | Gender |
|---|---|
|  |  |

H127. [If yes] How many days was the child under 5 sick with diarrhea, in the last 2 weeks?
Number of sick days (male child)_____[integer]
Number of sick days (female child)_____[integer]
Don't know_____998

H128. What do you consider to be the main causes of diarrhea?
[Single responses]
1. Dirty drinking water
2. Contaminated food
3. Wastewater and garbage
4. Muddy or flooded roads
5. Noise and sludge from factories
6. Weather
7. Other (specify)

**Question H128** is a broad attempt to link diarrheal illness to the source.

H129. Where or from whom do you seek advice or treatment when a family member is ill? [Multiple responses]

| | | |
|---|---|---|
| Friends, relatives, or neighbors | 1 (Yes) | 2 (No) |
| Pharmacy | 1 (Yes) | 2 (No) |
| Health center or clinic | 1 (Yes) | 2 (No) |
| Traditional doctor, healer, or practitioner | 1 (Yes) | 2 (No) |
| Referral hospital | 1 (Yes) | 2 (No) |
| Private doctor | 1 (Yes) | 2 (No) |
| Social media/internet | 1 (Yes) | 2 (No) |
| Other (specify) | 1 (Yes) | 2 (No) |

H130. How much total time was spent by all household members in seeking treatment for diarrhea and other water-related illnesses (e.g., amoebiasis, typhoid fever, cholera, dysentery, gastroenteritis) in the last 2 weeks? [Include the time spent at a health-care facility and/or pharmacy, including travel time.]
No. of days_____[integer]
Don't know_____998

**Questions H129–H138** address the treatment-seeking and treatment-providing activities of household members, and the health expenditures these activities incur (H131). They also address the opportunity costs due to the time spent caring for someone or spent at home while sick (H132–H138).

The reduction in the time and costs due to sick days or caring for a sick household member would be seen as a benefit of the reduced incidence of diarrhea and other water-related illnesses, and would thus be counted as health expenditure savings and income savings.

H131. How much did the household spend on medical treatments and medicines for diarrhea and other water-related illnesses in the past 2 weeks? [Include any spending on home remedies, such as special foods, drinks, or herbs.]

| | |
|---|---|
| Consultation fees | ₱/last two weeks |
| Medicines | ₱/last two weeks |
| Food | ₱/last two weeks |
| Transportation | ₱/last two weeks |
| Other (specify) | ₱/last two weeks |

H132. Did anyone in the household miss out on school days or workdays in the past two weeks due to diarrhea or other water-related illness?
1. Yes, missed school days
2. Yes, missed workdays [Skip to H134]
3. Yes, missed both school days and workdays
4. No [Skip to H135]

H133 [If yes] How many school days did any household members miss in the past two weeks?
No. of days_____[integer]
Don't know_____998
[Skip to H135 if no household members missed any workdays due to diarrhea and water-related illnesses]

H134. [If yes] How many days of work did any household members lose in the past two weeks?
No. of days_____[integer]
Don't know_____998

H135. Did anyone in your family spend time caring for household members who were sick with diarrhea and other water-related illness in the past two weeks?
1. Yes
2. No [Skip to H139]

H136. [If yes] Who usually takes care of the sick members of your household?
1. Female adult
2. Male adult
3. Female child
4. Male child

H137. How many days was the usual caregiver absent from school in the past two weeks due to time spent caring for household members suffering from diarrhea or other water-related illnesses?
No. of days_____[integer]
Don't know_____998
Caregiver does not attend school_____999

H138. How many days was the usual caregiver absent from work in the past two weeks due to time spent caring for household members suffering from diarrhea or other water-related illnesses?
No. of days_____[integer]
Don't know_____998
Caregiver does not work_____999

## Section 5: Flooding

H139. How frequently does flooding occur in your yard?
  1. Every time it rains
  2. Only when it rains heavily
  3. At least once a year
  4. At least once every 2 years
  5. At least once every 5 years
  6. At least once every 10 years
  7. Never

In this section, **questions H139–H140** establish the frequency of flooding on the respondent's property. **Question H141** looks at the depth of the flooding, and **question H142** looks at the duration.

H140. How frequently does flooding occur inside your house?
  1. Every time it rains
  2. Only when it rains heavily
  3. At least once a year
  4. At least once every 2 years
  5. At least once every 5 years
  6. At least once every 10 years
  7. Never

[If the answers to questions H139 and H140 are both "never," the survey ends here.]

H141. How deep is the average flood in your yard? [Ask respondents to indicate against their shin, knee, waist, etc., the water level in order to estimate or measure the depth of the flood.]
  1. 20 centimeters (cm) or less
  2. Greater than 20 cm to 30 cm
  3. Greater than 30 cm to 50 cm
  4. Greater than 50 cm to 100 cm
  5. Greater than 100 cm

H142. How long does the average flood last in your yard?
No. of hours_____[integer]
Don't know_____998

H143. In the past 12 months, have you experienced any damage to your property due to flooding?
1. Yes
2. No [Skip to H147]

**Questions H143–H155** look at the costs incurred by households due to flooding, including property damage (H144), income loss (H148–H149), loss of school days for children (H150), and other economic losses (H153).

Note: To aid in memory recall, reference could be made to a landmark flooding event or typhoon that occurred in the area during the past year.

H144. [If yes] How much did it cost to repair the damage to your house?
₱ (pesos)_____
[integer]
Don't know_____998
Did not repair damage_____999 [Skip to H147]

H145. How did you finance the repairs in your house? [Multiple responses]

| | | | |
|---|---|---|---|
| Own money (e.g., savings) | 1 (Yes) | 2 (No) | Skip to H147 |
| Flood insurance coverage | 1 (Yes) | 2 (No) | |
| Money borrowed from friends and/or relatives | 1 (Yes) | 2 (No) | [If no] Skip to H147 |
| Bank loan or credit card | 1 (Yes) | 2 (No) | |
| Money borrowed from a government agency | 1 (Yes) | 2 (No) | |
| Donations from friends and/or relatives | 1 (Yes) | 2 (No) | Skip to H147 |
| Donations from a government agency or nongovernment organization (NGO) | 1 (Yes) | 2 (No) | |
| Other (specify) | 1 (Yes) | 2 (No) | |

H146. If you borrowed the money, how much was the monthly repayment (which could include principal and interest)?
₱ (pesos) per month_____[integer]
Don't know_____998
No monthly repayment_____999

H147. Do the local schools and/or workplaces close when flooding occurs?
1. Yes, local schools only
2. Yes, workplaces only
3. Yes, both
4. No

This subsection also looks at how the household raised money to repair the damage to their houses caused by flooding during the past year (H145 and H154). This includes monthly loan repayments (H146 and H155).
The benefits provided by infrastructure investments aimed at flood prevention can thus be measured in terms of the avoided damage to property and livelihoods.

H148. How many days during the past 12 months have household members been unable to work because of flooding at home or at the workplace?
No. of days_____[integer]
Don't know_____998 [Skip to H150]
Did not miss work_____999 [Skip to H150]

H149. How much income per day did your household lose because of absence from work due to flooding?
₱ (pesos) per day_____[integer]
Don't know_____998

H150. How many days in the past 12 months have household members been unable to attend school because of flooding at home or on the school premises?
No. of days_____[integer]
Don't know_____998
Did not miss school_____999

H151. In the past 12 months, did your household experience economic losses due to flooding?
1. Yes
2. No [End of the survey]

H152. If yes] Which economic losses due to flooding did your household experience? [Multiple responses]

| Loss of land | 1 (Yes) | 2 (No) |
|---|---|---|
| Loss of crops | 1 (Yes) | 2 (No) |
| Loss of livestock | 1 (Yes) | 2 (No) |
| Other (specify) | 1 (Yes) | 2 (No) |

H153. If yes] Which economic losses due to flooding did your household experience? [Multiple responses]

| Loss of land | ₱/last 12 months |
|---|---|
| Loss of crops | ₱/last 12 months |
| Loss of livestock | ₱/last 12 months |
| Other (specify) | ₱/last 12 months |

H154. How did you pay for the economic losses that your household incurred due to the flooding? [Multiple responses]

| | | | |
|---|---|---|---|
| Own money (e.g., savings) | 1 (Yes) | 2 (No) | End of the survey |
| Flood insurance coverage | 1 (Yes) | 2 (No) | |
| Money borrowed from friends and/or relatives | 1 (Yes) | 2 (No) | [If no] End of the survey |
| Bank loan or credit card | 1 (Yes) | 2 (No) | |
| Money borrowed from a government agency | 1 (Yes) | 2 (No) | |
| Donations from friends and/or relatives | 1 (Yes) | 2 (No) | End of the survey |
| Donations from a government agency or nongovernment organization (NGO) | 1 (Yes) | 2 (No) | |
| Other (specify) | 1 (Yes) | 2 (No) | |

H155. If you borrowed money, how much was the monthly loan repayment (which could include principal and interest)?
₱ (pesos)/month _____[integer]
Don't know_____998
No monthly repayment_____999

## *Menstrual hygiene management (optional questions)*

H156. During your last menstrual period were you able to wash and change in privacy while at home? [applied to women who had periods during the preceding year]
  1. Yes
  2. No

H157. During your last menstrual period, what hygiene materials did you use?
  1. Cloth/reusable sanitary pads
  2. Disposable sanitary pads
  3. Tampons
  4. Menstrual cup
  5. Toilet paper
  6. Underwear alone
  7. Other (specify)

H158. Were these materials reusable?
  1. Yes
  2. No
  3. Don't know

H159. How did you dispose of used hygiene materials?
1. Thrown in the garbage
2. Flushed or put in the toilet
3. Buried or burned
4. Other (specify)

H160. During your last menstrual period, did you miss any of the following activities due to your period? [Ask one by one]

| | | |
|---|---|---|
| Attending school | 1 (Yes) | 2 (No) |
| Engaging in paid work | 1 (Yes) | 2 (No) |
| Participating in social activities | 1 (Yes) | 2 (No) |
| Cooking food | 1 (Yes) | 2 (No) |
| Eating with others | 1 (Yes) | 2 (No) |
| Bathing in regular place | 1 (Yes) | 2 (No) |
| Other (specify) | 1 (Yes) | 2 (No) |

# References

Ajuriagogeascoa, Nerea, Guy Norman, Wolf Schmidt, and Jonathan Stokes. 2018. *Citywide Surveys of Water and Sanitation Service Levels: Design and Methodology*. London: Water & Sanitation for the Urban Poor (WSUP).

Asian Development Bank (ADB). 2017. *Guidelines for the Economic Analysis of Projects*. Manila: ADB.

ADB and Egis. 2020. *KoboCollect: Data Collector Methodology*. Manila: ADB, Southeast Asia Urban Service Facility.

Brahme, Radhika, Sheela Godbole, Raman Gangakhedkar, Kuldeep Singh Sachdeva, Vinita Verma, and Arun Risbud. 2018. "Use of Computer-Assisted Personal Interviewing and Information Management System in a Survey among HIV High-Risk Groups in India: Strengths, Weaknesses, Opportunities, and Threats Analysis." *Indian Journal of Community Medicine* 43 (2): 107–12.

Creative Research Systems. Online sample size calculator.

DataSpring editors. "7 Common Questionnaire Mistakes Market Researchers Should Avoid." dataSpring (blog). 4 April, 2018.

Egis. 2020. *Survey Data Collector: A Compilation of the Kobo Toolbox Support User's Guide*. Manila: ADB, Southeast Asia Urban Service Facility.

Food and Agriculture Organization (FAO). n.d. "Chapter 4: Questionnaire Design." Accessed 7 July 2021.

Garcia, Adrian. 2014. "Summary of Standardized Usability Questionnaires." *LinkedIn*, 28 November 2014 .

Gibson, Michael, and Ben Morse. n.d. "Data Quality Checks." Abdul Latif Jameel Poverty Action Lab (J-PAL). Accessed 7 July 2021. https://www.povertyactionlab.org/resource/data-quality-checks.

Gunatilake, Herath, Jui-Chen Yang, Subhrendu Pattanayak, and Kyeong Ae Choe. 2007. "Good Practices for Estimating Reliable Willingness-to-Pay Values in the Water Supply and Sanitation Sector." ERD Technical Note Series No. 24. ADB, Economics and Research Department (ERD), Manila, December.

Humans of Data. 2017. "How to Conduct a Successful Focus Group Discussion." 11 September.

Hyman, Michael, and Jeremy Sierra. 2016. "Guidelines for Writing Good Survey Questions." *NMSU Business Outlook*, 14(2). pages 1-10.

Raosoft. Online sample size calculator. Accessed 8 July 2022. http://www.raosoft.com/samplesize.html.

Sajise, Asa Jose, Jindra Nuella Samson, Lotis Quaio, Jasmin Sibal, David A. Raitzer, and Dieldre Harder. 2021. *Contingent Valuation of Nonmarket Benefits in Project Economic Analysis: A Guide to Good Practice*. Manila: ADB.

Sullivan Gail M, and Anthony Artino Jr. 2017. "How to Create a Bad Survey Instrument". *Journal of Graduate Medical Education*, 9(4):411-415.

SurveyMonkey. Online sample size calculator.

SurveyMonkey. "5 Common Survey Question Mistakes that'll Ruin your Data." SurveyMonkey (blog). Undated.

Tonthat, Kris. 2019. "Common Mistakes of Survey Design." DisplayR (blog). 21 February, 2019.

United Nations Children's Fund (UNICEF)/World Health Organization (WHO). 2018. *Core Questions on Drinking Water, Sanitation and Hygiene for Household Surveys: 2018 Update*. New York: UNICEF and WHO.

United Nations Department of Economics and Social Affairs. 2016. Integrating a Gender Perspective into Statistics. Studies in Methods, Series F No. 111. New York: UN.

UNICEF. n.d. "Household Questionnaire." Multiple Indicator Cluster Survey (MICS). Accessed 15 March 2021.

Whittington, Dale. 2002. "Improving the Performance of Contingent Valuation Studies in Developing Countries." *Environmental and Resource Economics,* 22 (1): 323–67.

World Bank. n.d. "Economics of Sanitation Initiative." Water and Sanitation Program. Accessed 18 May 2021.

www.ingramcontent.com/pod-product-compliance
Lightning Source LLC
Chambersburg PA
CBHW061255230426

43662CB00028B/2455